Higher-Consciousness Healing

Discover Your Personal Healing-Symbols to Solve All Your Problems

by
Tara Springett

Copyright 2020 Tara Springett
All rights reserved
ISBN: 9798689643397
Imprint: Independently published

Contents

Acknowledgements 5

Introduction 6

Chapter 1 What kind of problems can be solved with Higher Consciousness Healing? 11

Chapter 2 Who can work with Higher Consciousness Healing? 17

Chapter 3 How did Higher Consciousness Healing come into existence? 22

Chapter 4 How does Higher Consciousness Healing work? 26

Chapter 5 Defining our problem 49

Chapter 6 Measuring our suffering on a scale 58

Chapter 7 Relaxing our body and mind 63

Chapter 8 Opening up to our Higher Consciousness 69

Chapter 9 Exploring our life-path 74

Chapter 10 Asking for a healing-symbol 85

Chapter 11 Working with our healing-symbol 94

Chapter 12 Working with our healing-symbol for two weeks 118

Chapter 13 Getting feedback on our process 132

Chapter 14 Working through complex problems 138

Chapter 15 Using Higher Consciousness Healing for making decisions 143

Chapter 16 Maintaining well-being in every area of our life 147

Chapter 17 The ultimate healing-symbol 152

Chapter 18 Manifesting our dreams 155

Chapter 19 Practising Higher Consciousness Healing on behalf of others 162

Chapter 20 Teaching Higher Consciousness Healing to others 168

Chapter 21 The complete practice of Higher Consciousness Healing 171

About the author 177

Acknowledgements

First of all, I want to thank all my Buddhist teachers and in particular Rigdzin Shikpo and Garchen Rinpoche. They guided me safely around all the pitfalls that lay on the spiritual path and taught me how to find love first in myself and then with others. Deepest thanks to Wally Sawford who is a very special Buddhist and Taoist teacher. He helped me to have meditation experiences which inspired me greatly.

I want to thank all my psychotherapeutic teachers, most of all Phyllis Krystal from whom I learnt about the amazing effectiveness of symbols in the therapeutic process. Thank you to all my clients who had the trust and the courage to try a new method and who shared their processes with me. Lots of thanks to Richard Sylvester who enthusiastically explored all the possibilities of Higher Consciousness Healing with me and helped a great deal in writing the first version of this book.

Thanks to my wonderful husband Nigel who readily tried Higher Consciousness Healing as soon as I discovered it and supported me in every respect. Without his generous help, this book would not have been written.

Introduction

In 1997, I had an experience that changed my life for ever. I was sitting in the shrine-room of my Buddhist teacher trying to listen to his talk but I could not concentrate because I was inwardly struggling with a painful feeling of sadness that had been bothering me for many years. As I had often done before, I prayed for help and – lo and behold! – this time my prayer was fulfilled. Suddenly, the method described in this book just 'popped up' in my mind. It was so clear and detailed that I assumed I had read it somewhere and was just remembering it. In the weeks and months that followed, I successfully used this method to dissolve my sadness and many smaller issues, as well.

    I then introduced this method to my friends and family and later to my clients. I carefully monitored their individual processes and asked everybody to measure their success on a scale. The results were overwhelming. I have worked with many hundreds of cases and virtually *every single person* who has used this method has achieved significant improvements with a wide variety of problems within a few days or weeks. Also, many people have given me the feedback that they achieved wonderful results all by themselves simply by learning the method from this book. Most importantly, these improvements were stable and lasting. Higher Consciousness Healing seems to have the power to transform personal problems without lengthy analysis and without having to go back to the past.

    When I look back, it seems as if much of my life had been leading up to this experience and had prepared me to 'receive' this method, refine it and, further, make it accessible to other people. Thirteen years earlier, I had found Tibetan Buddhism like a lost child running into their mother's arms. It was a true experience of coming home and since the very first day I visited the Buddhist centre, I have meditated every day for at least an hour. I spent virtually all my vacations in intensive teaching and meditation retreats with knowledgeable and experienced teachers who guided me along the way. Over the years, a deep motivation evolved in me: I wanted to develop so much happiness, insight and love that I could be of *real* benefit to other people.

A few years after I had started to meditate, I began to work as a counsellor and psychotherapist and tried to put my desire to help other people into practice. I had completed several long-term counselling training courses, had gained qualifications and I felt that my ability to help had grown considerably. However, after working for the first few years, I started to wish I could find a technique that was more effective in helping my clients than that I had been using so far. Ideally, the method should be very simple so that everyone would be able to use it as a self-help tool. It should also bring reliable results *every* time it was used. Also, my ideal method should point people to the eternal truth that true happiness can only be found through the awakening of a loving heart.

When I 'discovered' Higher Consciousness Healing, I had no idea that it would fit this wish exactly in all its aspects. Only when one person after another gained very good results with this method did I become slowly convinced that I had been given a real gem.

The core of Higher Consciousness Healing is making contact with our Higher Consciousness – which is the part of our mind that is more loving and wise than our everyday consciousness. If we follow a spiritual path, we may choose to perceive our Higher Consciousness as the central figure of the religion we follow. However, we do not need to be religious or spiritual to benefit from Higher Consciousness Healing. The essence of our Higher Consciousness is altruistic love, a form of love that is available to everyone no matter whether they are spiritual or not.

Higher Consciousness Healing will help us to communicate with our Higher Consciousness and make its wisdom and love available to solve our personal problems. We receive this help through the use of symbols. These symbols – when visualised regularly for just four minutes a day – have an amazing power to transform our problems. They can reach deep into our unconscious mind and put things right at their root. We do not even need to know all the intricate causes of our problem because in Higher Consciousness Healing we focus entirely on the solution. The practice is absolutely safe and we can achieve a significant decrease in our suffering with almost every problem in a matter of days or weeks. This may sound exaggerated – but it is true.

Ellen's results are a good example and demonstrate the sometimes stunning transformative power of Higher Consciousness Healing. Ellen had been suffering from depression, social phobia and low self-esteem almost all her life. She had been in and out of psychotherapy, counselling and self-help groups for over fifteen years. Her depression had improved when we met but she still suffered terribly from her social phobia and low self-esteem. I asked her to measure her suffering on a scale from zero to ten (zero is no suffering at all and ten is utter desperation) and she said that she was at seven. This meant that she felt strong and painful anxiety every day in many different situations.

Ellen agreed to try Higher Consciousness Healing and I guided her into relaxation. She chose to see her Higher Consciousness in the form of a beautiful, bright light and received a purple gem as a healing-symbol. I then explained to her how she should visualise her symbol in the middle of her heart and breathe out its good qualities with love to herself and to the people she was afraid of. Unfortunately, Ellen was not very optimistic.

'I do not expect instant results,' she said seriously.

'Okay,' I said. 'Just give it a go.'

Two weeks later, Ellen and I spoke on the 'phone.

'My anxiety has decreased from 7 to 1 on the scale,' she said but she still wasn't very impressed. 'I definitely feel better,' she told me, 'but I cannot believe it is this symbol. I probably feel better because it is the holiday.'

'Just try it for another two weeks,' I said smiling inwardly. I had experienced her reaction myself – sometimes, the results of Higher Consciousness Healing are too good to believe.

Two weeks later, Ellen came to my practice 'Tara,' she said, 'I am zero on the scale and I have never been zero before in all my life. The holiday is over and I even had a terrible argument with my daughter's doctor. Normally, that would have left me shattered. But I am still fine. I am cross with the doctor but happy with myself.' Ellen has remained well. Sometimes, her old fears wanted to resurface but when she remembered her healing-symbol, she could return to her positive state of mind in a very short time.

Higher Consciousness Healing is based on the principles of Tibetan Buddhism but the technique in itself is new and unique. It can be used by anyone who feels inspired by it and it will not interfere with the practice of other religions or spiritual beliefs. It is a short and simple method that can be learned and practised within minutes.

Even though Higher Consciousness Healing is a very simple practice, it regularly brings great improvements to even the severest problems. I have worked with clients who had been sexually abused as children and clients who had been raped as adults and violently assaulted. I have worked with people who have suffered all their lives from panic attacks, addictions, clinical depression, violent anger, chronic pain and debilitating tiredness. I have also worked with many couples on the brink of divorce, desperate parents and children suffering from many problems. To my joy, *they all, virtually without exception,* experienced dramatic and lasting improvements by using Higher Consciousness Healing within days or a few weeks.

Chapter 1
What kind of problems can be solved with Higher Consciousness Healing?

Higher Consciousness Healing was initially developed as a method of transpersonal psychotherapy and it was intended to be used for emotional problems or relationship issues. But it turned out that Higher Consciousness Healing works equally well with other problems like addiction, financial worries, physical pain, spiritual blocks and fatigue. Here is a non-exhaustive list of problems one can tackle with Higher Consciousness Healing.

Anxiety
Depression
Stress
Sadness
Anger
Frustration
Loneliness
Bereavement
Addiction
Alienation
Lack of confidence
Eating disorder
Low self-esteem
Feeling easily dominated and overwhelmed
Desperation
Feeling traumatised
Feeling weighed down by responsibility
Grief and hurt

Compulsive behaviour
Guilt-feelings
Problems in making decisions
Being too dominant and controlling
Shock
Problems and stress in relationships
Physical pain
Weight problems
Exhaustion
Tiredness
Sexual problems
Lack of direction in life
Problems to do with work and career
Confusion
Financial problems
Problems in achieving what you want
Energy blocks
Psychic domination
Being stuck or confused on the spiritual path

The effect of Higher Consciousness Healing on others

Higher Consciousness Healing *always* has a positive effect on the people who are involved in our problem. This is because the core of the practice is altruistic love. Sometimes, the people who are involved in our problem change in ways that we never thought possible. But it is important to note that this influence does not come from our mind with all its little egotistical concerns but from our Higher Consciousness which always works in the highest interest of everyone involved. Therefore, Higher Consciousness Healing will lead us to a solution to our problem that will reduce the suffering of *everybody* involved in the best and healthiest way possible. The following case study shows these effects quite clearly.

Case study: Susan

Susan was married to a man who was verbally abusive to her on a regular basis. I helped Susan to receive a healing-symbol from her Higher Consciousness and showed her how to send love to herself and her husband by enveloping them both in bubbles of loving, joyful light. In her mind, she said to him, 'I wish you to be happy' and imagined that he would be very loving if he was happy. Susan had initially thought that the solution to her marriage problem was to become more tolerant of her husband and 'learn not to be hurt anymore'. However, after practising Higher Consciousness Healing for a few days, Susan did something that she had never considered doing before and told her husband in clear terms that she would leave him if he didn't change his ways. At the same time, she was much kinder to him than before and started to cuddle him for the first time in years. To her joyful surprise, her husband gave up his abusive language and they both started to talk honestly about their feelings. After another three weeks, they were also able to rekindle their sex life. These improvements were stable and lasting.

The effect of Higher Consciousness Healing on our physical body

Obviously, Higher Consciousness Healing is not a replacement for any medical treatment. However, I have seen in many cases that it can greatly enhance the effects of good treatment. It has particularly shown great effectiveness in reducing physical pain and chronic tiredness. One of the therapists who I trained in Higher Consciousness Healing is a massage therapist. She gave me a long list of well-documented case studies that show how Higher Consciousness Healing has helped her clients in reducing their various forms of pain. The following case study shows the effectiveness of Higher Consciousness Healing on our physical body.

Case study: Val

Val had had extremely painful periods for over twenty years. She had tried all kinds of treatment without any lasting success and had resigned herself to the fact that she had to take a handful of strong painkillers every month. Val felt really inspired by Higher Consciousness Healing and started practising at once. When she had her next period, she found to her amazement that her pain had reduced so much that she only needed one single painkiller. Encouraged by this success, she carried on with her visualisation and in the following months, she didn't need any painkillers at all. From then on, Val stopped her visualisations and has remained pain-free ever since.

Using Higher Consciousness Healing to help others

Higher Consciousness Healing is an excellent method to help others who are in psychological or physical pain. I have seen particularly impressive improvements when parents have used Higher Consciousness Healing to alleviate the suffering of their children. Here is an example:

Case study: Philippa (mother) and Imogen (7 years)

Imogen suffered from extreme shyness that was so bad that her teachers suspected that she was deaf. Philippa transferred Imogen to a Montessori school but, unfortunately, her condition did not improve. Philippa then learnt Higher Consciousness Healing and started to send love to her daughter with the help of a healing-symbol. To Philippa's great surprise, Imogen's shyness dramatically lessened within days of doing this practice. Imogen even started to play with other children, which was something she had never done before. Imogen's condition continued to improve over the following months.

Summary

Higher Consciousness Healing can be used for all personal problems.

People who are involved in your problem might change in amazing ways but it is not your personal will that brings about these changes. They are brought about by your Higher Consciousness, which always acts in the highest interest of everyone concerned.

Higher *Consciousness Healing is very effective in reducing physical pain and chronic tiredness.*

Higher *Consciousness Healing can be used to help others very effectively.*

Chapter 2

Who can work with Higher Consciousness Healing?

The best help anyone can offer is to give people an effective tool that they can use to solve their problems themselves. Higher Consciousness Healing is such a tool. It is a self-help method designed for people who are interested in an effective way of solving their problems with a minimum of cost, time and energy. Anyone who feels inspired by such a method can work with it.

Higher Consciousness Healing is so simple and so safe that most people can easily learn it from this book and practise it on their own without the help of a therapist. Over the years, I have had many emails from people reporting their positive results from this method and thanking me. However, most case studies in this book come from my own life-coaching practice because I was able to monitor these cases more carefully and convince myself that the improvements were real. The following case study is about a man who used Higher Consciousness Healing all by himself.

Case study: Andy

After one of my talks about Higher Consciousness Healing, a man approached me and told me how he had overcome his depression simply by reading this book and doing the exercise. It was not difficult for Andy to receive his healing-symbol by asking his Higher Consciousness in relaxation. He received a red ruby and visualised the symbol in his heart whenever a low mood crept up on him. Andy felt the loving light of his symbol fill his body and mind and it comforted his hopeless spirit. Gradually, he felt better and better. When he spoke to me, he had been free of depression for six months.

There are very few prerequisites for using Higher Consciousness Healing. You do not need to be spiritual or religious to use Higher Consciousness Healing – you simply need to trust that there is a part of your mind that is more loving and wise than your everyday self. However, if you are religious or spiritual, you can use your beliefs to practise this method without altering anything about them.

Quite a few people are concerned that they cannot visualise. Fortunately, the kind of visualisation we need in Higher Consciousness Healing is so basic that anyone can do it. For example, look at a small object in front of you and study all the details. Now close your eyes and describe the object. If you can do this, you can visualise enough to use Higher Consciousness Healing effectively. You do not need to 'see' everything as clearly as if you were looking at it on the television. It is enough to think of your symbol or to just 'know' what it looks like. You can also make a simple drawing of your symbol and look at this image without visualising anything at all.

Some people are afraid that Higher Consciousness Healing may bring up upsetting memories or a healing crisis (things getting worse before they get better). Fortunately, this is not at all the case. In all the years that I have been using Higher Consciousness Healing, I have found this method to be completely safe as well as extremely pleasant to practise. One big advantage of this method is that it will *not* bring up distressing memories or upsetting material.

Higher Consciousness Healing is so simple that it can even be used by children (usually from four years of age onward) and I have regularly seen dramatic improvements in their physical and psychological well-being. Equally, it can be used by parents *on behalf* of their smaller children. In fact, I have noticed that Higher Consciousness Healing works particularly quickly when it is used on behalf of or by children.

Case study: Thomas

Thomas is the nine-year-old son of one of my clients. His mother taught him the simple practice of Higher Consciousness Healing and every day they practised together their respective symbols. Thomas's first symbol was geared at improving the relationship with his stepfather. He was so successful that his stepfather remarked positively on the improvements even though he didn't know anything about the practice. Then Thomas received a symbol to overcome his shyness at school and promptly felt a lot more confident. His mother told me that Thomas continued to use Higher Consciousness Healing whenever he felt a problem arising – which was greatly empowering for him.

Unfortunately, I have observed that not everyone wants to solve their problems in such a quick and effective way. In my holistic life-coaching practice, I have found that people can be very attached to their problems. On the surface, they maintain that they want to get better but, in reality, they are much more interested in trying to convince me that their problem is not solvable. Some people even feel offended if you tell them that there is a method that can rid them of their problems in a very short time and that their suffering does not need to be explored in depth. They react as if you want to take something very precious away from them.

Another obstacle is that some people believe that they need to find a trauma from their past that has caused their present problem in order to solve it. If I tell these people that this search is unnecessary and that their problem can be solved much faster, some of my clients are a bit resistant.

In other cases, people have remained sceptical even if they had impressive improvements with Higher Consciousness Healing. Unfortunately, the rational part of their mind could not accept the gift that this method really is and they dismissed its healing power. Also in other cases, people felt sad after they had been very successful with Higher Consciousness Healing. For example, Barbara (who you met in the introduction) was almost upset after she successfully dissolved her social phobia and asked, 'Why did I have to go through all those years of therapy when it could have been so easy?' I cannot answer this question other than sharing my feeling that Higher Consciousness Healing is a wonderful gift that we just did not receive earlier.

Summary

Higher *Consciousness Healing is an effective self-help tool designed for people who are interested in solving their problems with a minimum of time, money and energy.*

You do *not need to be religious or spiritual to use Higher Consciousness Healing. You can view your Higher Consciousness simply as the part of your mind that is more loving and wise than your everyday consciousness.*

Everyone *has enough basic visualisation skills to use Higher Consciousness Healing effectively. It is enough to think about your symbol or to simply know that it is there.*

Higher *Consciousness Healing is a very straightforward method and is completely free of side effects. No upsetting traumas from the past will come up and no healing-crisis is to be expected.*

Chapter 3
How did Higher Consciousness Healing come into existence?

At the time that I 'discovered' Higher Consciousness Healing, I had been suffering for many years from a subtle but deep feeling of emotional hurt and sadness that seemed completely disconnected from what was going on in my life. This feeling would just not go away no matter how much my life improved on the outer level and no matter how much I worked on my inner being with various therapeutic methods and intensive Buddhist meditation. I had tried everything: psychoanalysis, bio-energetics, past life regression, aromatherapy, crystal therapy, emotional freedom technique (EFT), cognitive-behavioural therapy, Landmark education, mantra chanting, brain hemisphere synchronisation, Taoist energy work and bodywork. But no matter what I did, the sadness always returned.

I felt very frustrated but something inside told me that it was possible to solve my problem just as I had solved many other problems in my life. So, I fervently wished that my suffering should not be in vain and that I would be able to use my problem to discover the deepest principles of personal healing in order to help other people. I believe my desire to use my suffering to help others was one of the reasons that my prayer was answered by my 'discovering' Higher Consciousness Healing. My pain has truly been like the grit in an oyster that finally produced a beautiful, precious pearl.

Working with symbols was not new to me because, in my work as a holistic life coach, I had been treating clients for years using the therapy developed by Phyllis Krystal that she described in her book *Cutting the ties that bind*. Her approach also uses symbols but, in a different way to Higher Consciousness Healing, Krystal does not help her clients to receive their *own* symbols and she does not use love in the healing process.

In the first year after discovering Higher Consciousness Healing, I refined the method by using all the knowledge I had gained from my many years of training in Buddhism and psychotherapy. Sometimes, I had a strange feeling – as if an unseen force was guiding me in this process. For example, my symptoms sometimes flared up for no clear reason and this led me to try refining my approach to Higher Consciousness Healing. After I had made these improvements, my symptoms disappeared as quickly as they had come. Over time, Higher Consciousness Healing brought me a degree of harmony, peace and happiness that I had never experienced before.

After I and some of my friends had experienced very good results with Higher Consciousness Healing, I felt no hesitation in adding the practice to my counselling repertoire when working with my clients. Higher Consciousness Healing proved so effective that two things happened. Firstly, I dropped almost all the other techniques that I had learnt in my Gestalt therapy training, family therapy training and body awareness therapy training in favour of Higher Consciousness Healing. Secondly, the length of time my clients spent with me in therapy shortened dramatically. Often they felt 'sorted out' after only a few sessions.

Using Higher Consciousness Healing makes people much more independent so that they do not need the help of a professional so much or even at all. This is because, through

Higher Consciousness Healing, people can quickly learn to rely on the help of their own inner resources.

Case study: Sue
Sue contacted me because she wanted to find a partner. She felt lonely, depressed and very fearful that she would never find someone. We first worked on her fear, which she successfully decreased with the help of a healing-symbol. But Sue still felt depressed and lonely. Therefore, her next symbol was geared towards her depression and her negative self-talk such as, 'It's not meant to be' or 'It's hopeless'. After practising her new healing-symbol for another two weeks, Sue told me that she had been able to stop her negative self-talk and that she felt altogether more positive and trusting. Simultaneously, she went on many blind dates. In the past, Sue had found blind dates depressing and exhausting but now she saw them as a positive learning experience. When I last spoke to her, all her depression and fear had gone and her loneliness had been replaced with a sense of faith that she would soon find someone.

Summary
The method *of Higher Consciousness Healing method just 'popped into' in my mind while I was praying for help for a longstanding emotional problem of my own. My problem improved significantly in a matter of days.*
I refined *the practice and introduced it to my friends and, later, my clients.*

Higher *Consciousness Healing proved so effective that the number of sessions my clients spent with me dropped dramatically.*

Chapter 4
How does Higher Consciousness Healing work?

A century ago, Sigmund Freud developed his now-famous model of the superego, the ego and the id. The conscious ego, Freud argued, struggles to keep the antisocial drives of the id and the strict and limiting demands of the moralising superego at bay.

This model and many of Freud's other theories were hailed as great advances in our understanding the human psyche. Many forms of psychotherapies that were developed after Freud still use his basic ideas to explain how emotional disturbances come about and how they can be cured. Unfortunately, Freud's model of human nature does not give much hope for deep happiness because his model does not recognise that there is a vast potential of positive qualities that lies within each of us.

The personality model in Higher Consciousness Healing

Higher Consciousness Healing is based on a model that is significantly different from Sigmund Freud's and it has three main parts:

the conscious mind (also called the everyday or personal mind)
the unconscious mind
the Higher Consciousness (also called one's Higher Power)

Our conscious mind encompasses everything that we are aware of. This includes our sense perceptions, feelings, thoughts and memories. Although some of us like to think that the conscious mind is the largest part of the human mind, it is actually the smallest. It is like the tip of an iceberg while the unconscious mind is like the large part of the iceberg beneath the water. The unconscious mind is many times bigger than the conscious mind because it contains all our past experiences in minute detail and it also contains everything we are experiencing at the moment but are not aware of. This may include background noises that we blank out or feelings and thoughts we do not want to deal with at the moment. The unconscious mind is neither negative nor positive in itself. It is more like the storehouse of all the internal and external experiences we have ever had.

Between the conscious and the unconscious mind there is a semi-permeable boundary. That means that certain things that have been conscious can become unconscious and other things that have been forgotten can become conscious again. If you want to experience how things can become conscious, you can try thinking about what you ate yesterday...and the day before yesterday...and the day before that. If you are like most people, you will not remember what you ate for more than two or three days ago. When you cannot remember any further back, the door between your conscious and unconscious mind has closed. This closed door between the conscious and unconscious mind is the major problem in any kind of psychotherapy that relies on recollecting old traumas to heal the patient. I will say more about this problem later but first I would like to finish explaining the model of the human mind.

The role of the Higher Consciousness

By far the biggest part of our mind is our Higher Consciousness because it is unlimited and permeates the entire universe - including the minds of every being. In this respect, we cannot talk about our Higher Consciousness as something personal or individual. Our Higher Consciousness is something we share with every other being in the universe. It is outside of us and something other than what we think we are, yet it is also inside of us and is the core of our being. Most of us are unaware of the presence of our Higher Consciousness and every genuine spiritual path aims to make us fully aware of it.

It is difficult to imagine the vastness of our Higher Consciousness because it is more than our conscious mind can understand. Also, the notion that we all participate in an all-encompassing mind can seem like an insult to our personal ego that wants to believe that we start and end where our body starts and ends and that we are separate and highly individual beings.

No matter how hard we try to understand our Higher Consciousness, we cannot fully grasp it because, ultimately, it is a mystery. We come across the idea of something mysterious and all-encompassing in most religions. Christians call it the Holy Spirit and Buddhists call it Buddha-nature. In this book, I call it Higher Consciousness so that people of all backgrounds can work with it. And, as I mentioned before, you do not need to be spiritual to benefit from Higher Consciousness Healing.

So what is our Higher Consciousness like?

Imagine for a moment that you feel utterly free, up-lifted and without limitations. Nothing burdens you, no worries constrict you and joy fills your heart. You feel you have access to unlimited knowledge and infinite possibilities and you can do whatever you want. Now imagine that this vast space of freedom is filled with the sweetest and most tender love flowing freely from your heart to all beings without discrimination. All notions of friends and enemies have gone and you can love everyone alike. You can see that other people are suffering and deepest compassion springs from your heart as you see them struggling. But you can also see the way to happiness with complete clarity and you realise that all the negative ways in which people behave come from their misguided search for happiness. You feel only one deep wish and that is to remove all the suffering that people are experiencing and show them the path to true happiness.

Can you imagine all this? These feelings and this wisdom will grow stronger as we develop the awareness of our Higher Consciousness. However, our Higher Consciousness is more than I have just described – much more. The love, compassion and wisdom of our Higher Consciousness are infinite and without boundary. It truly goes beyond the limits of our imagination. Yet it is our true nature – it is what we ultimately are. So, how can our Higher Consciousness help us to solve our problems? I have to go back a little bit to explain this.

The dangers of making unconscious material c onscious again

You have probably noticed that many problems – and in particular emotional problems – cannot be solved through merely thinking and talking about them. Obviously, it is nice to let off steam and receive some sympathetic support but this alone will not solve our problem if an essential part of it is unconscious. On the contrary, our problem can seem to become even bigger the more we think and talk about it. It is like zooming in on an issue until nothing else exists – but still without finding a solution. Therefore, to solve our psychological problems we need to find a way to work effectively with the part in us that is causing the problem but is unconscious at the moment. One way of doing this is to enter a type of psychotherapy that tries to uncover unconscious material.

Several forms of psychotherapy work on the assumption that emotional or psychosomatic problems are caused by traumatic experiences from the past. These can be in our childhood or even our previous lives. Typically, in these approaches, it is believed that we have to make this traumatic material conscious again to release old negative feelings and correct any unhealthy decisions that we made at that time.

Let me illustrate this with an example. A woman who has problems creating committed relationships enters psychotherapy. By working with her unconscious mind, she is regressed to the age of three and discovers that she was sexually abused. According to the theory, she can now release her suppressed feelings of anger and grief and thus become happy and successful.

Different therapies use different methods to regress the client and make the unconscious conscious. Unfortunately, bringing up unconscious material can have severe side effects. The regression method does not acknowledge that there is a very good reason why we have become unconscious of the terrible traumas from our past. It is one of the most merciful qualities of our mind that it can forget the bad things from our past so readily. If you are over thirty years old, you have probably noticed that your past seems better and better the older you become. This ability of our mind to forget many of the painful things helps us to concentrate on our lives in the present and be free of the burdens of our past. People who cannot forget the traumas they have experienced suffer from post-traumatic stress that can make their present life a living hell. They need help to *forget* the dreadful things they have experienced.

When we dig into our unconscious mind to release old traumas, it can sometimes be utterly devastating. Some people who discovered during psychotherapy that they had been sexually abused as children have reported that their recollections were as distressing as if they had been sexually abused again. Instead of releasing old negative emotions, they were swamped and overwhelmed by them.

It is very difficult to deal with recollections like these. They can be extremely painful to bear and they can make you feel like a victim. To make matters even worse, there is no way of telling whether these 'memories' are true mirrors of reality. If we carefully investigate what is actually happening in any form of regression therapy, all we find are 'pictures in the mind'. Nobody can say for sure what these pictures really represent. Are they true recollections? Are they fantasies? Or are they a mixture of both?

Imagine that you discover in regression that you felt neglected as a baby. What do you do with this 'memory`? It is very difficult to go to your mother and ask her about it. In all likelihood, she will be hurt by your questions and deny everything. But one thing is sure, it will make your relationship with your mother much more difficult.

How our Higher Consciousness can solve our problems

Fortunately, Higher Consciousness Healing can deal with the part of our problem that is unconscious in a way that is completely free of these risks. With Higher Consciousness Healing, we do not need to remember any traumas and we do not need to uncover anything distressing. It does not matter if the cause of a problem is related to our childhood or even a past life. We do not need to know any of that. Any searching for the cause of a problem will make our problem appear bigger while not solving anything at all.

'But how can I solve a problem if I do not even know its cause?' you might ask.

The answer is that knowing the cause of a problem will not necessarily lead us to its solution. *And it is the solution to the problem that we need to find, not its cause!*

This is where our Higher Consciousness comes into play. Albert Einstein famously stated that 'No problem can be solved from the same level of consciousness that has created it'. This quotation points to the core of Higher Consciousness Healing. Instead of diving deeply *into* our problems, we need to jump *out* of them by accessing a part of our mind that is more loving and wise than our everyday mind – a part that already knows the solution. This part our mind is our Higher Consciousness. Since our Higher Consciousness penetrates our entire mind including our unconscious mind and because it is ultimately wise and loving, it already knows the solutions to all of our problems. If we can access the wisdom of our Higher Consciousness, we do not need to make unconscious material conscious - we can go for the solution straightaway. By the way, once we know the solution to our problem, we often find that we have discovered its cause, as well.

How symbols can heal problems that are rooted in our unconscious mind

The big challenge at this point is how to communicate with our Higher Consciousness. Most of us only have occasional glimpses of our Higher Consciousness. Traditionally, meditation and prayer are the only ways to deepen our experience of our Higher Consciousness. Fortunately, Higher Consciousness Healing offers us a way of communicating with our Higher Consciousness even if we have never meditated before.

Language is not very suitable for this communication because words are much too crude to communicate with higher forms of wisdom and compassion. What we need is something that will bridge the gap between our relatively crude personal mind and our Higher Consciousness. This bridge can be created with the help of symbols.

The idea of using symbols to communicate with our Higher Consciousness is not new. Most religions give us symbols to help us make this contact. In Higher Consciousness Healing, you will receive your own symbols to solve your problems. It is important to understand that symbols are more than just little pictures or statues. They are charged with the energy and meaning of what they are meant to communicate and they really do embody what they symbolise. So in effect, the symbol and what the symbol stands for cannot be separated – they are one.

With symbols, we can work in three different ways. Firstly, we can make contact with our Higher Consciousness by visualising it in symbolic form. For example, some people choose to see their Higher Consciousness as a shimmering light or as an angelic being while others stay with the well-known images from traditional religions. Secondly, our Higher Consciousness can send messages to us in the form of healing-symbols. Thirdly, we can focus on these healing-symbols in order to send messages deep into our unconscious mind. In our unconscious mind, information is usually stored in the form of pictures rather than in words. For this reason, language does not work very well as a means of communicating with this part of our mind, either. Using symbols is much more effective and gives our unconscious mind the information it needs to transform.

When we repeatedly give all parts of our mind a message from our Higher Consciousness in the form of a symbol, we can achieve amazing results. New and healthy ideas arise, negative emotional patterns decrease and tiredness disappears. We might also find that our life circumstances begin to change mysteriously. This process is safe, free of side effects and, best of all, extremely effective. With Higher Consciousness Healing, you can work on problems that have their roots deep in your unconscious mind without ever getting the undesired side effects of trying to uncover unconscious material.

'Wait a minute,' I can hear you say, 'it cannot be that easy! Surely you have to work with your problems at least a little bit!'

You are right. You need to work with your problem – but not in a negative or self-destructive way. Unfortunately, many people think that self-development only works when there is pain, crisis or suffering involved. This is untrue. Personal development can be completely free of pain – but only if we have the skilful means to achieve this. We need a solution-oriented approach that will create positive feelings, new possibilities and new insights. Higher Consciousness Healing is such an approach.

How Higher Consciousness Healing compares to positive thinking

In Higher Consciousness Healing, we assume that the root of all problems comes from having (unconscious) faulty beliefs about ourselves and the world. Beliefs like 'I am not loveable' or 'women are not trustworthy' create negative emotions and bodily tensions, which in turn can lead to neurotic or physical symptoms. Higher Consciousness Healing works on the level of these deep beliefs but in a very different way than positive thinking.

Traditional forms of positive thinking work by replacing our negative beliefs simply by repeating the opposite positive affirmation as often as possible. For example, if someone thinks, 'I am stupid' they should simply replace this thought with, 'I am intelligent' and repeat it constantly. Unfortunately, our negative beliefs will often not go away that easily. On the contrary, positive thinking can easily degenerate into a constant struggle to keep our inner negativity at bay. We may even get on the nerves of our friends because they quickly sense that our 'positiveness' is not that genuine. Unfortunately, by trying too hard to think positively, we often experience even more painful self-denial and separation from others.

In Higher Consciousness Healing, we do not use words at all but simply introduce our inner being to a beautiful *image* that radiates love in all directions. Doing this will not evoke the inner resistance that we often encounter when we try to *think* positively. However, it is nevertheless important to stop tormenting ourselves with negative self-talk. Calling ourselves a 'fat cow' or 'stupid idiot' always evokes negative feelings and our healing-symbol can be used to cut through this inner negativity. The following case study shows how this looks in practice.

Case study: Janice
Janice contacted me because she suffered from depression. Once we talked about her feelings in more detail, it turned out that she blamed her mother for her depression because she did not feel properly cared for as a child. At the same time, Janice (who was also a counsellor) recognised quite clearly that, in fact, she had had quite a loving upbringing. Therefore, her first symbol was geared at resolving her negative relationship with her mother and Janice sent love to herself and her mother with the help of a healing-symbol for two weeks daily. The results that this brought about were very surprising for Janice, who had been in and out of therapy for decades. Suddenly, she felt more liberated and happy than she ever been before and she had a genuine love for her mother for the first time in years.

However, Janice still suffered from the bad habit of constantly comparing herself unfavourably with others, which made her feel envious and resentful. I talked to Janice about the importance of stopping this negative self-talk and learning to be her own best friend. From then on, Janice made a great effort to stop her unfavourable comparisons by firmly placing her mind on her symbol and its loving light. As a result, her resentment and envy gradually disappeared.

The healing power of love

The essence of our Higher Consciousness is love. It is this infinite and unconditional love that radiates out from our healing-symbol and produces the often miraculous improvements with Higher Consciousness Healing. *Therefore, the most important aspect of Higher Consciousness Healing is to focus on the love that shines forth from our beautiful symbol and allow this love to penetrate all our problems.* Love is the sincere wish for oneself and others to be happy.

When we work with a healing-symbol, we first let its loving light shine towards ourselves and wish ourselves to be happy from the bottom of our heart. Doing this will remove all forms of self-loathing and raise our self-esteem to a healthy level.

In the next step, we let the loving light of our symbol shine out to all the people who are involved in our problem and we wish them to be happy, as well. It may seem very difficult to send love to the very people who have harmed us but I have seen with all my clients that it can be done quite easily when we are supported by a healing-symbol from our Higher Consciousness. Sending love is a positive intention rather than a feeling of infatuation or attraction. We simply have to imagine that if our adversary was genuinely happy, they would immediately regret all the bad things they have done and become a very likeable person, instead. Doing this has tremendous healing power. The following case study demonstrates how Kathy freed herself from the terrible effects of sexual abuse by using this approach.

Case study: Kathy

Kathy (32 years) had been sexually abused as a child by her uncle. She was full of self-loathing, depression and hated her uncle with a vengeance. Kathy's biggest problem was that she never had a single loving encounter with a man, which made her very unhappy. I explained to Kathy that I was optimistic that she could find true love even though she had suffered sexual abuse as a child. In my opinion, her biggest obstacle to finding love was the current hatred that she felt towards herself and her uncle and not the abuse itself.

Kathy understood what I was trying to say but felt that to stop hating her uncle was like taking away his guilt. I said to Kathy that nobody could take away the guilt of her abuser and that he had to live with it for the rest of his life. What we were trying to do was to liberate Kathy by cutting the ties of hatred that bound her to her uncle. 'Love will set you free,' I said, 'resentment will tie you to your abuser. Love means wishing your uncle to be happy in the knowledge that this would make him into a good person who intensely regrets what he has done. It does not mean liking him or taking away his guilt.'

After we had talked all this through, Kathy was willing to give it a try. For the first two weeks, she sent the healing light of her symbol only to herself and experienced a sense of happiness and purity that was completely new and wonderful for her. Then she bravely began to send the light of her healing-symbol to her uncle (who she visualised a very long distance away) and wished him to be happy and loving. As she was doing this, she suddenly had a strong feeling that her uncle had been sexually abused as a child himself and she even felt a little bit of compassion for him. At that moment, Kathy truly felt free from all the negative effects of the abuse for the first time in her life. Most wonderfully, after practising in this way for a few weeks and feeling better and better in herself, Kathy happily fell in love for the first time in her life with a very supportive and loving man.

Love is the supreme healing power in the universe. To be healed from the effects of trauma, neglect and abuse, we do not need to go back to our initial experiences. It is wonderful to see that *all* negative feelings resulting from past traumas can be effectively dissolved by sending love to ourselves and our perpetrator with the help of a healing-symbol. It is not the memories themselves that make us suffer but our *current* resentment and victim mentality. By using the healing power of love, painful emotions will subside, physical ailments will heal more quickly and wisdom will arise to help us solve our conflicts more constructively.

Additionally, sending love to others often produces real and positive changes in these people – even if the other person does not know anything about our practice. I have seen numerous cases where difficult people have positively transformed when my clients sent love to them with the help of a healing-symbol. Below is another case study that demonstrates the powerful effect of Higher Consciousness Healing on others.

Case study: Harriet

*Harriet had many problems (depression, loneliness, inability to find a partner) that she blamed on her father who had been in a mental care home from the time she was a child. Harriet told me in elaborate detail how her previous therapist had shown her that her current relationship problems were all due to her growing up with a mentally ill father. 'I hate my father,' she told me with tears in her eyes. I told Harriet that I didn't share the opinion of her previous therapist and that I believed that it was her **current** resentment towards her father that accounted for her emotional problems. I then showed her how to send love to herself and her father with the help of a healing-symbol and to say to her father in her mind, 'I wish you to be happy and healthy.'*

The effect of this practice was immediate. Harriet felt as if a big burden had fallen off her chest and her life-long feeling of depression virtually disappeared within days. After doing this practice for several weeks, Harriet told me with joy that the mental health of her father had improved so much that he had been able to leave to hospital for the first time in years. She then asked me if I thought that this was caused by her practice of Higher Consciousness Healing. I said to Harriet that there was no proof that her father's improvement was due to her practice but that I was not surprised at all because I had regularly seen similar improvements with Higher Consciousness Healing. Both Harriet's and her father's improvement remained stable.

The role of relaxation in Higher Consciousness Healing

Every single negative emotion – depression, anger and fear – has a corresponding area of tension in our physical body. For example, many people feel depression as a sensation of painful tension in their chest or head; anger as tensions in legs and arms and anxiety as a tense knot in their stomach or neck. People tend to have unique but stable patterns of tensions that go along with their negative emotions. Once we know our personal form of tensions and become able to deeply relax these parts of our body, our negative emotions will be gone. It is as simple as that! Focusing on the loving light of our symbol and letting it penetrate the areas of our tensions make this process very easy and effective.

The role of correct breathing in Higher Consciousness Healing

When we focus on our healing-symbol, we let its colour radiate out in synchronicity with the *out-breath*. The whole focus in Higher Consciousness Healing is always on the out-breath and never on the in-breath. The reason for this is that focusing on breathing out makes people more relaxed while focusing on breathing in makes them more tense. In this way, breathing correctly can calm down all sorts of negative emotions and is particularly effective when we work with anxieties and fears. With a healing-symbol and the correct form of breathing, even panic attacks can be alleviated in a matter of a few minutes. In my holistic life-coaching practice, I have had many clients suffering from chronic fear, anxiety and panic. They all, without exception, could free themselves entirely from these negative emotions within a matter of a few days or weeks by focusing on their healing-symbol and breathing correctly.

The role of visualising bubbles of love

When we send love in Higher Consciousness Healing, we imagine that this love forms bubbles of loving, joyful light around ourselves and others. These bubbles are roughly as big as our outstretched arms and have a firm boundary. Visualising these firm boundaries can give people a much greater sense of inner security. It also helps to clarify difficult relationship entanglements.

Generally speaking, most relationship problems are due to two main dynamics: people are either too submissive and allow themselves to be dominated by others or they are too egotistical and drive people away through their overbearing behaviour. Both problems are due to unhealthy ego boundaries. Self-sacrificing (co-dependent) people give up their ego boundaries and are unhealthily merged with more dominant people. On the other hand, people who are too selfish do not respect the ego boundaries of others and impose their own will on the people around them. Generally speaking, most people who seek therapy belong to the first category and have problems with confidence and saying 'no'.

In Higher Consciousness Healing, the healthy ego boundaries of each person are symbolised through firm bubbles of loving, joyful light that emerge from our healing-symbol and surround ourselves and another person who is involved in our problem. These two bubbles may touch if we wish but they should never overlap and merge. A merging of these bubbles of light would symbolise an unhealthy fusion of people who do not dare assert themselves or who treat each other in an overbearing way. By repeatedly visualising beautiful bubbles of loving, joyful light around ourselves and others, we can easily establish healthy ego boundaries no matter whether we belong in the submissive or dominant personality category. Doing this is incredibly powerful and often restores clarity and love in complex relationship problems in a matter of days or a few weeks. The following case study demonstrates how Gillian's marriage improved even though her husband knew nothing about Higher Consciousness Healing.

Case study: Gillian
Gillian came to see me because she felt she was on the brink of divorce from her husband of sixteen years. She complained bitterly how he had no respect for her and treated her 'like a cleaner'. When I suggested that she should ask her husband to tidy up his stuff, she explained that she was too scared to do this because her husband would get angry very easily. Her response sounded so negative that I personally doubted that her marriage could be rescued. However, after Gillian had visualised them both within two bubbles of love with the help of a healing-symbol for two weeks, things improved dramatically for them. Gillian became able to ask her husband for what she needed and to her great surprise, her husband became amenable to her requests to tidy up his stuff. As a result, the atmosphere between the two of them became quite loving. These improvements continued to deepen and stabilise in the months that followed.

I want to mention here that I always work towards maintaining a marriage except in cases of violence or unaddressed addiction. In these cases, I always urge the couple to separate.

The role of colour in Higher Consciousness Healing

The healing-symbol that we receive from our Higher Consciousness needs to have a bright and beautiful colour. It is well-known that bright colours have a strong effect on people's moods and physical well-being. For example, trains are often decorated in soothing blue to stop people from vandalising them and new-born babies suffering from jaundice are effectively treated with nothing but a bright orange light. Interestingly, in terms of effect, it does not make any difference if colours are real or imagined.

In Higher Consciousness Healing, we use the healing effect of colour by flooding our body and surroundings with the beautiful, bright light that radiates from our healing-symbol. Doing this further enhances the effectiveness of the practice and brings about profound changes in psychological and physiological well-being.

The role of smiling in Higher Consciousness Healing

Higher Consciousness Healing is an altogether positive approach that completely dispenses with rummaging through our old traumas and painful emotions. Instead, we immediately go to the solution to the problem - including feeling joyful and happy. Therefore, when we focus on our healing-symbol, it is very helpful to jumpstart feeling positive by gently smiling. In the beginning, this smile may feel a bit strained but most people quickly find that it helps them to regain a good mood more readily. This is particularly true for people who suffer from sadness and depression. Once people feel better in themselves, they are more able to solve their various problems.

Case study: Holly
Holly (29 years) contacted me because she had suffered from depression all her life. This painful feeling had started at the age of ten when her parents took her to India where Holly could not cope with the sight of abject poverty. In contrast to traditional counselling, I did not ask Holly to relive her painful memory but instead asked her where in her body she felt her sense of depression. After introspecting for a little while, Holly discovered that her depression felt like a black rock in her brain. I then guided Holly to send love to herself with the help of a healing-symbol and to smile gently to herself. Simultaneously, she tried to 'relax the black rock in her brain' with every out-breath by seeing it opening out like a beautiful flower. Within ten minutes, Holly's continuous feeling of depression was gone. However, once Holly went home she couldn't completely maintain this happier state. When she came back after two weeks, she reported that her depression was better but not gone. The 'black rock' in her brain felt now like 'grey smoke'. Once again, I guided Holly through the process of Higher Consciousness Healing and from then on her depression was completely gone.

Does Higher Consciousness Healing merely suppress our problems?

Some readers may be concerned that Higher Consciousness Healing is just a powerful way to suppress negative emotions. Fortunately, this is not at all the case. I have had many opportunities to meet my clients months, even years, after working with them and I ask them if they have been able to maintain their improvements. To my joy and delight, virtually everybody reported that their improvements had been lasting and stable. Further, I did not find any signs that the initial problem had been replaced by different or more severe problems. In general, people were led by Higher Consciousness Healing to a genuine and healthy solution and lived an altogether better life.

Case study: Ron

One of my clients, Ron, tried Higher Consciousness Healing because he had had problems in his relationship with his wife for a long time. They both felt dissatisfied and their relationship had been chugging along without any significant highs or lows. When Ron tried Higher Consciousness Healing, he expected everything to simply get better. But instead, something happened that was quite atypical for him. He suddenly felt an urge to sit down with his wife and discuss all the little problems and irritations that had accumulated over the years and this urge grew and grew. Talking about their problems was the very thing that Ron and his wife had avoided throughout their relationship. They had both always been afraid that any kind of argument might mean the end of their relationship. But to his astonishment, Ron noticed that his fear of discussing problems significantly decreased. So he asked his wife to talk with him and she agreed. Their conversation was not nearly as difficult as Ron had expected and they found compromises that worked much better than their usual silent, half-grudging arrangements.

After all this explanation, you might still wonder how exactly Higher Consciousness Healing brings about all these wonderful results. I have to admit that I do not have an answer to this question. The deeper working principles of Higher Consciousness Healing remain inexplicable just like any other question that touches on the primordial ground of our being. Higher Consciousness Healing works by connecting us to the source of deepest love and wisdom in the universe and this source will always remain a deep mystery. In the same way, the dramatic improvements of well-being from using Higher Consciousness Healing cannot be explained from a purely rational or psychological point of view. Something much deeper is at work here and we need to value these forces to harvest their full results. So you need a little faith to give Higher Consciousness Healing a serious try. Let's get started!

Summary
Our Higher *Consciousness penetrates our entire unconscious mind and can change our problem at its root. We do not even need to know the cause of our problem.*
In Higher *Consciousness Healing, there is no risk of upsetting, traumatic material coming to the surface as happens in many forms of therapy that work with regression.*

The most *effective way to communicate with our Higher Consciousness and our unconscious mind is through symbols rather than through words.*

By far *most the important aspect in Higher Consciousness Healing is the love that radiates from your healing-symbol – first to ourselves and then to everyone who is involved in the problem. Loving someone means wishing this person to be happy.*

If we can *send love to our negative emotions and difficult people around us, our problems will be genuinely dissolved.*

It is not *the actual traumas from our past that make us suffer but our current resentment and victim mentality. Once these negative attitudes have been dissolved with the help of a symbol, we will be free to fulfil our dreams.*

In Higher *Consciousness Healing, we use relaxation, correct breathing, the visualisation of bubbles surrounding us, colour therapy and smiling to support the healing process.*

Chapter 5
Defining our problem

The first and most important step in Higher Consciousness Healing is to define our problem precisely and correctly. If the definition of our problem is broad and vague, the effects of Higher Consciousness Healing will also be broad and vague. The more precisely we can point to the core of our problem, the more effectively Higher Consciousness Healing will work.

When I started to train people as practitioners in Higher Consciousness Healing, I found that many of my students were almost addicted to over-analysing problems and trying to find 'deeper layers'. My clients often do the same. Many of them try to explain to me all the underlying causes of their problems to the extent that I start wondering whether they are the psychotherapist or me! However, when we use Higher Consciousness Healing, we do not need all this 'psychologising'. In fact, too much 'deep' analysis of our problem is not only superfluous but makes things unnecessarily confusing. In any case, it is often impossible to know the underlying reasons for our problems because they are stored safely away in our unconscious mind. Too much analysing is often no more than guesswork, which makes the whole process vague again.

Pinpointing negative emotions

The core of every problem – no matter how complex and complicated – are our **current negative emotions.** Many people who come to my life-coaching practice tell me long stories about all the aspects of their problems. However, in terms of solving their problem, I only need to know one thing: *what the most* *painful emotion connected to the problem is.* Once I know the negative emotion, I can go straight to helping my client receive a healing-symbol and then letting their Higher Consciousness do the rest of the work. Unfortunately, it is easy to get confused when we are confronted with all the intricate aspects of a problem. The best way to clarify the situation is to cut through all these ideas and simply ask ourselves, 'which negative feeling do I experience most often when I suffer from this problem? Is it most like anger, most like sadness or most like anxiety?'

To get the best results from Higher Consciousness Healing, we must always work with the emotion that is causing us the most suffering at the moment. For some people, this is very easy to do and they will know very clearly that they are mostly anxious or depressed, for example. However, there are quite a few people who are not really in touch with their emotions and find it difficult to name what they are feeling. For them, the following three columns can be very helpful. These three columns show that there are three main categories of negative emotions – anger, sadness and anxiety. Virtually all painful emotions belong to one of those categories.

Anger (directed at oneself or others)	Sadness	Anxiety
irritation	depression	nervousness
frustration	grief	fear
impatience	feeling down	panic
boredom	emotional hurt	stress
disgust	despair	time pressure
grudges		embarrassment

revulsion resentment self-loathing bitterness hatred self-hatred		shyness worry

Feelings like jealousy, envy and greed belong to one of these categories as well, depending on whether they are a more angry form of this feeling or a more anxious or sad form. For example, in greed, anxiety (about missing out) can be the most predominant feeling or anger (about having missed out).

If we find difficulty in pinpointing our negative emotion, we can ask ourselves: *is my negative feeling most like anger, most like sadness or most like anxiety*? Knowing the main category of our feeling is usually enough to get good results with Higher Consciousness Healing. Let us assume we suffer from stress at work; it is not enough to define our problem simply as stress. Is our stress most like anger, sadness or anxiety? Once we know our negative feeling, we can define our problem in the following way:

'my suffering from feeling (emotion) about...'.

Let me give you an example. Maybe you are one of the many people who suffer from being overweight and would like to shed some pounds. It is not enough to define your problem as 'suffering from being overweight'. If you want to use Higher Consciousness Healing for this problem, you need to ask yourself: What exactly do I *feel* when I experience the suffering from being overweight? Is my feeling most like anger, sadness or anxiety? Not everybody feels the same negative emotions about the same problem. Some people may be depressed about their weight while others may be really frustrated (anger category). If you feel emotions from two categories (for example, self-loathing and fear) you need to decide which of these feelings is more painful and work with the strongest emotion first. For example, if self-disgust (anger category) is your worst emotion, you can define your problem as 'my suffering from feeling disgusted about my body'.

If you have a problem which has many different emotions (like a divorce, for example), you should always start with the most painful emotion. Later, you can work through the different layers of emotions with different symbols. Please see Chapter 14 about how to work through complex problems.

Sometimes, people tell me that they are not suffering from negative emotions but that they have an unfulfilled wish. If they only had a partner or a job, they say, they would be happy. However, in every situation in which we feel unhappy, we also find negative emotions. If someone wishes for a partner, for example, they might be suffering from feeling sad or frustrated. If someone is unemployed, they might suffer from worry or depression. If we use Higher Consciousness Healing for problems like these, we might not find a job or a partner straightaway but we will definitely feel better in a genuine way. Once we feel happier, we will also be more successful in our search for whatever we wish for. Please see Chapter 16 for more details on wish fulfilment.

If we suffer from physical pain or fatigue, we can simply name our problem as 'suffering from feeling pain' or 'suffering from feeling tired'. Pain and fatigue are not emotions but defining our problem in this way works well.

Feeling the body-mind connection of negative emotions

Once we have named our negative feeling, we need to explore where our emotion manifests in our physical body. *All* feelings *always* have a physical aspect that manifests as tensions in various parts of our body. Knowing our unique pattern of tensing up helps us to dissolve our disturbing feeling more effectively later on in the process.

For some people, the body-mind connection is very obvious and they know straightaway that their anxiety feels like a big knot in their solar plexus, for example. However, for other people, emotional tensions are a new concept and they need some support to find the physical manifestation of their emotions. As a general guideline, anger often manifests in arms and legs, sadness or depression can often be felt in the chest, eyes or head while anxiety can often be felt in the solar plexus, throat and shoulders. However, it is important that you find your *own* pattern of emotional tensions in your body. Here is a little exercise to help you:

Feeling negative emotions in your physical body
For a *short moment, think of your problem and feel the main negative emotion that is associated with it (anger, sadness or*

anxiety). Once you feel the negative feeling, ask yourself: **Where** *in my body do I feel this negative feeling?*
Do not *worry if you cannot answer this question immediately. Instead, scan your body in search of your negative feeling. Start with your toes. Is the negative feeling in your toes? In your feet? In your ankles, knees, thighs, abdomen, around the waist, in your chest, shoulders, arms, hands, neck, face, eyes or head?*
If you *suffer from fatigue, do the same and look closely where in your body your sense of tiredness manifests.*

Once you have noticed where in your body you can feel your painful emotion, you can relax again and continue with the process of Higher Consciousness Healing. We will come back later to these emotional tensions and dissolve them.

The correct definition of the problem

Once we have named our negative emotion and explored the mind-body connection, we can define our problem in the following format:

'My suffering from feeling (emotion) about...'

In the many years of working with Higher Consciousness Healing, I have found that this form of problem definition brings the clearest feedback later on. Once we have clear feedback that Higher Consciousness Healing does work for us, we will be motivated to carry on with this approach. Here are some examples of how to define our problem and how not to.

Correct definition of your problem	*Incorrect*
My suffering from feeling afraid of my boss	My suffering from stress at work (too vague)
My suffering from feeling frustrated about my weight	My suffering from feeling fat ('fat' is not an emotion)
My suffering from feeling sad about not having a girlfriend	My problem is that I had a neglectful childhood and this is why I feel lonely now (over-analysis)
My suffering from feeling frustrated about not having enough money	My suffering from having no money (no emotion)
My suffering from feeling grief about the death of my mother	I want to be happy again (this is a wish)
My suffering from feeling angry about my arguments with my husband	My suffering from my husband's temper (you need to discover *your own* emotion)
My suffering from feeling depressed (if there is nothing specific that you feel depressed about, you can define your problem in this short way)	I suffer because I was abused (no emotion)
My suffering from feeling the pain of sciatica	My suffering from feeling the stress that has caused the sciatic pain (over-analysis)

| My suffering from feeling frustrated because I do not know which career to pursue | I am suffering because I haven't found my dream job yet (no emotion) |

Sometimes, people feel anxious or depressed about nothing in particular. If you experience this form of free-floating negative emotion, you can simply define your problem as, 'my suffering from feeling sad/anxious/irritable'.

In some cases, people worry that Higher Consciousness Healing may help them to get rid of their negative emotions but not 'solve their problem'. This worry is unfounded as the following case study will demonstrate.

Case study: Jane

Jane came to see me because she was depressed about her non-existent career. When I helped her to define her problem, she said that it was more important for her to find a job rather than simply feeling better. My answer was that if she was happier, she would be much more able to solve her problems. Jane, for example, was so depressed that she could not even get out of bed in the morning. Therefore, we defined her problem as, 'suffering from feeling depressed about my career'. She received a purple gemstone as a healing-symbol that helped her to decrease her depression to a good degree. Once she felt better, she was able to go to the jobcentre, write applications and cope with rejections.

Summary

The most *important aspect of the problem definition is your current negative emotion associated with your problem.*

There are *three main categories of negative emotions: anger, sadness and anxiety. Try to pinpoint which of these three emotions you feel when you experience your problem.*

Explore *where in your body you can sense your negative emotion. Knowing this will help you to dissolve your feeling later on.*

You need *to define your problem in the following way: 'My suffering from feeling (emotion) about...' without trying to guess what the underlying cause might be.*

Chapter 6
Measuring our suffering on a scale

In the next step, we need to measure our negative emotion associated with our problem on a scale from one to ten. Measuring negative emotions in numbers is something that is done in several forms of psychotherapy and is a powerful tool. In Higher Consciousness Healing, we use it to get feedback on the results of the method. I have often seen that people forget how bad their problem was after only two weeks of practising Higher Consciousness Healing. Unfortunately, this can lead them to dismiss the effectiveness of the practice. By comparison, if my clients receive proper feedback with the help of measuring their negative emotions on a scale, it increases their motivation to continue. The following story illustrates this point.

Case study: Zoe

At one of my talks, I guided everybody through the practice of Higher Consciousness Healing so that they could all try the method out. The whole group relaxed, made contact with their Higher Consciousness and received healing-symbols. Then I told everyone how to visualise their healing-symbol for the next two weeks. One person, Zoe, 'phoned me two weeks later about something that had nothing to do with Higher Consciousness Healing. After we had talked about this, I asked her how she had got on with her healing-symbol. Zoe told me that she had asked for a symbol to overcome her suffering from grief about her brother who had died recently. She admitted that she had not practised her healing-symbol for the required two-week period and that she had stopped as soon as she felt better. I reassured her that I did not mind at all and asked her whether she could remember what her grief had measured on the scale at the evening of the talk. For a moment, there was silence at the other end of the telephone. Then Zoe said, 'Tara, I cannot believe that I was suffering so much. I had completely forgotten how bad it was only two weeks ago. When I was at your talk, I felt my grief measured eight on the scale – my whole life felt like it was one big trauma. I feel so much better now. I would say my grief is no more than three on the scale.

When we rate our suffering on the scale, it is important to rate only our negative emotion and not 'the whole problem'. For example, if someone has defined their problem as 'suffering from feeling depressed about my weight', they should only rate the amount of their depression and not the amount of their weight-loss. Dissolving our negative emotions is the most important aspect of Higher Consciousness Healing because once someone feels happier, they will be much better at doing whatever they want - including losing weight. In the following chart, each number on the scale of suffering is explained in more detail.

Measure your negative emotion on the scale of suffering

Zero means that you do not experience any negative emotion at all. At zero, you do not have a problem.

One means that you feel a very slight negative emotion which hardly bothers you at all.

Two means that your negative emotion comes up every now and then but that you can still ignore it most of the time quite easily.
Three means that your negative emotion is hard to ignore any more. You are still happy most of the time but you feel you have to do something to solve your problem.
Four means that you suffer a good deal from your negative emotion although you can still switch off from your problem.
Five means that your negative emotion is so strong that it gives you a considerable amount of suffering and that switching off becomes quite hard.
Six means that switching off from your negative emotion becomes harder and harder. It bothers you most of the time and causes you a lot of suffering.
Seven means that you are starting to feel desperate.
Eight means that you are deeply unhappy. You experience almost nothing else but your negative emotion and you have only very little hope left.
Nine means that you are extremely desperate. You are completely engulfed by your negative emotion and you have lost all hope.
Ten means that you are completely and utterly desperate.

Some people make huge jumps down the scale of suffering within a few days of starting to use Higher Consciousness Healing. However, most people can expect substantial results after two weeks of practice. This is the reason I advise people to practice Higher Consciousness Healing for at least two weeks and then measure their results on the scale and compare this number with their first one. Most people will improve even further after another two to four weeks. They may also experience some smaller ups and downs within this time span. Even though four to six weeks is an extremely fast improvement for getting rid of a lifetime of neurotic symptoms, some people tend to stop any method that does not bring instant and complete results. In cases like this, it is very helpful to use numbers as an encouragement to keep going.

In some cases, people find it difficult to think about their emotions in numbers. This is understandable because our emotions come from the right half of our brain and our ability to think logically in numbers comes from the left hemisphere of the brain. It is not always easy to get the two hemispheres to work together. However, the more the halves of our brain are in harmony, the more effective and successful we can be as a whole person. Then we do not need to have different compartments for our emotional, intuitive and creative concepts on the one hand and our rational, analytical and logical concepts on the other. Instead, we can respond to every situation both emotionally and rationally at the same time. Using numbers to measure our negative emotions is a way of training ourselves to bring our two brain hemispheres together. It brings rational awareness to more emotional people and emotional awareness to more rational people.

Summary
Measure *how much you suffer from your negative emotion on a scale from zero to ten (zero is no suffering at all and ten is utter desperation). Only measure your negative emotion and not the 'whole problem'.*

Measure *your suffering again after you have practised Higher Consciousness Healing for two weeks and compare the results.*
Having *a clear feedback system will enhance people's motivation and encourage them to carry on with the practice.*

Chapter 7
Relaxing our body and mind

Once we have defined our problem and we have measured our negative emotions on a scale, we can start in earnest. To receive a healing-symbol, we need to contact our infinitely loving and wise Higher Consciousness. Our Higher Consciousness is the core of our being, our true nature and the true nature of the whole universe and yet we are rarely fully in contact with it. Someone who is truly one with their Higher Consciousness has transcended the human world – yet nobody will be more human. This person will be more humble and more compassionate than anyone else. They will be full of inspiring humour and have the deep wisdom to help others. Our Higher Consciousness is both the crown of human development and the way we transcend it at the same time. Why is it so difficult to be in more contact with our Higher Consciousness? If it is our true nature, why cannot we be more aware of it?

The biggest hindrance to recognising our Higher Consciousness is fear. This is a very deep and basic fear that we all carry around with us even if we are not aware of it. It is this fear that motivates most of our thoughts and actions and fuels our constant questions such as 'How can I get what I want? Am I being supported? How can I get rid of the things I do not like? How can I stop being invaded and controlled by others?' We might not be very conscious of these questions nor of the fear that lies behind them and yet they control how we tackle most situations in our life.

If we were in complete union with our Higher Consciousness, all these questions would cease to exist and we would be completely trusting. There would be nothing but a constant flow of love and joy and the natural wisdom that enables us to do whatever is beneficial for everybody. Someone who is in contact with their Higher Consciousness is so happy that they have energy and genuine concern for others – naturally and effortlessly.

When we become more aware of our Higher Consciousness, we also develop more real confidence in ourselves. This is not the same confidence we see in arrogant and self-centred people. True confidence makes our heart open and compassionate and makes us very modest in a happy way. When we lose our basic fears, we do not need to think about ourselves all the time. It genuinely does not matter anymore how we look, how much money we earn and what others think of us. We are just too happy to be bothered about things like that. The challenge is how to overcome our deep fears and be closer to our Higher Consciousness.

The best antidote to fear is relaxation. It is impossible to experience fear in a deeply relaxed body and mind because fear is nothing else than tension. You have probably noticed how tense your body becomes when you are really afraid, how your breathing becomes fast and shallow and how your mind cannot stop thinking about the very thing that is making you afraid. If you could lay down, relax your whole body, practise slow breathing and let go of the stressful inner images, your anxiety would disappear within minutes.

To work with Higher Consciousness Healing, we do not need to be able to relax very deeply. For most people, a little bit of relaxation is quite enough and can be achieved by following one of the suggested relaxation methods in this book.

Some people have a relaxed body but a very tense mind while others have a relaxed body and a sleepy mind. Neither state is desirable for Higher Consciousness Healing. The ideal we are aiming at is a relaxed body and a calm but alert mind.

If you have practised relaxation exercises before, you can use whatever relaxation method suits you best. In the overview of Higher Consciousness Healing at the end of the book, you will find a reliable and effective method of relaxation. If you find that this form of relaxation does not work for you, here are two alternative methods.

Relaxation method A
Sit or lie *down comfortably and undo any belt or tight clothing.*
Let yourself *become aware of the rhythm of your breathing. Imagine you are sitting on a sledge and every time you breathe out, you slide down a gentle, snowy mountain slope. As your out-breath finishes, your sledge comes to a gentle standstill at the bottom of the hill. Be aware of the gap before you find yourself breathing in. Allow this gap to lengthen as long as is comfortably possible. Gently breathe in again and then see yourself sliding down the gentle mountain slope as you breathe out. Gently lengthen the gap at the end of each out-breath. Carry on breathing like this for a few moments.*
Tense the *muscles in your feet as you breathe in and when you breathe out release all the tension in your feet. Tense the muscles of your calves and then release them with your next out-breath. Continue in this way and tense and then release the muscles of*

your thighs, stomach, chest, shoulders, arms, hands, neck, face and head.
Imagine *you are sitting on a beautiful cloud and you are sailing gently towards a wonderful place of your choosing - like a beach or a garden. When you arrive at this beautiful place, climb down from your cloud and sit or lie down somewhere where you feel comfortable.*
Enjoy your *deep relaxation.*

Relaxation method B
Sit or lie *down comfortably and undo any belt or tight clothing.*
Feel your *right leg becoming more and more relaxed. Feel your left leg becoming more and more relaxed. Your right arm becomes more and more relaxed and so does your left arm. Your whole body becomes more and more relaxed.*
Now your *right leg becomes comfortably warm. Your left leg becomes comfortably warm. Your right arm becomes comfortably warm and so does your left arm. Finally, your whole body becomes comfortably warm.*
See yourself *drifting through an endless, open space. You feel wonderful in this space. You are surrounded by love and happiness and you feel free and liberated.*
Now you *see a beautiful, bright light in the distance. You feel drawn to this light and you move nearer and nearer to it. Finally, you enter the radiant light and it surrounds you with pure love. You merge with this light and then you move through it. When you have passed through the light, you find yourself in a beautiful place. It might be a garden or a beach or a beautiful house.*

***Find a place** to sit or lie down comfortably and enjoy your relaxation.*

In some cases, Higher Consciousness Healing can produce results that resemble miracles. I am reluctant to take any credit for these 'miracles' and I am just deeply grateful that they occur. The next case study demonstrates a miraculous improvement in the health of ten-year-old Harry.

Case study: Amy and Harry
Amy, the mother of ten-year-old Harry, contacted me in deep concern because her son was seriously ill with colitis (chronic inflammation of the large intestine). He had stopped growing and, at the time, his condition was so severe that he was hospitalised and fed through a nose tube. I helped Amy receive a healing-symbol on behalf of her son - it was the image of an angelic being in a long, white robe. Amy was very happy about this symbol. She went home and showed her mother and her husband how to practise Higher Consciousness Healing and they all visualised the angelic being radiating with love in Harry's heart. To their great delight, the boy made such a quick recovery that it stunned his doctors. After a very short time, he was allowed to leave the hospital and was able to return to school. A little while later, his parents found a new and side-effect-free medication that improved his health even further.

Summary

The biggest *obstacle to making contact with your Higher Consciousness is a basic fear that everyone carries around with them.*

A relaxed *body and a calm but alert mind help us to experience more of our Higher Consciousness and receive healing-symbols.*

Chapter 8
Opening up to our Higher Consciousness

Our Higher Consciousness is the nature of the universe and also the nature of ourselves. In its essence, it is infinite space imbued with love, wisdom and bliss. For most people, it is easiest to visualise their Higher Consciousness in a personified form like an angelic being that is infinitely loving and wise. Doing this is probably not very difficult for people who hold religious beliefs. To practise Higher Consciousness Healing they can simply visualise the central figure of their religion and open their heart to this divine being.

People who do not have any spiritual beliefs can think of their Higher Consciousness as the part of their mind that is more loving, happy and wise than they feel at the moment. They may choose to see it simply as a shimmering light. Everyone else can choose to visualise their Higher Consciousness in whatever form is inspiring for them, for example, as an angelic being, a wise old man or as a living and loving light, as long as their inner image is really beautiful.

In my counselling practice, I have found that there is only one form of visualisation that does not work well and that is imagining that our Higher Consciousness looks like ourselves. Even though our Higher Consciousness is the essence of ourselves, we tend to miss its vast power by visualising it looking like ourselves.

You may ask how our Higher Consciousness can take all these different forms. The answer is that we always perceive our Higher Consciousness from our personal point of view depending on our culture, belief system, upbringing and religious background. This personal context determines both the way we perceive the world and the way we perceive our Higher Consciousness. There is nothing wrong with this and Higher Consciousness Healing will work in whatever form we perceive our Higher Power. However, even though our Higher Consciousness can appear in many forms, it does not mean that people 'own' their personal Higher Power. We all share our Higher Consciousness because it is the nature of the universe.

For Higher Consciousness Healing to work, we do not have to have a mystical vision of our Higher Consciousness. If our Higher Consciousness does not appear spontaneously in our front inner eye, we can simply choose how we want to imagine it. For example, many of my clients like to perceive their Higher Consciousness as a shimmering light that has a living and deeply loving quality. *It is always important to visualise our Higher Consciousness in a beautiful colour and surrounded by brilliant, radiant light.*

In whatever form we perceive our Higher Consciousness, we need to remember that our Higher Consciousness *is always wise and loving and never critical or judgmental.* If our Higher Consciousness seems to be criticising us or anybody else, we should think that the channel to our Higher Power must be blocked. The critical voice that we hear is actually the voice of our own personal consciousness. When this happens, we simply need to relax a little more and try again.

'But how can I know that I am perceiving my Higher Consciousness correctly and that I am not making it up?' you might ask.

The answer is that most of us will always perceive a mixture of our Higher Consciousness and our own consciousness. On a 'good day', we will perceive more of our Higher Consciousness and on a 'less good day' we may perceive more of our own consciousness. This is absolutely normal and does not decrease the effectiveness of Higher Consciousness Healing. To use this method, we do not need to be an advanced spiritual seeker. All we need is to have the wish to open up to our Higher Consciousness. At the end of the day, the only thing that matters is that Higher Consciousness Healing brings results in a straightforward way.

Once we are in contact with our Higher Consciousness, we need to ask for help. Asking for help can be difficult for some of us because it means admitting that we are not as strong and self-sufficient as we would like to be. However, to gain the full benefit of the help of our Higher Consciousness, we have to give up the idea that we are completely autonomous and in control. Even though our Higher Consciousness is the essence of ourselves, we need to perceive it as something higher and stronger than ourselves; otherwise, we cannot really open up to its enormous power. The help of our Higher Consciousness is the most beautiful gift in the universe and we need some humility in order to receive it gratefully.

Case study: Alison

Alison contacted me because she felt very lonely and longed to find a partner. Her most painful emotion was sadness and she received a healing-symbol to overcome this feeling. I showed Alison how to send love to herself with the help of her healing-

symbol and envelop herself in a comfort blanket made of the loving light of her symbol. At first, Alison found this hard and she recognised that she had the neurotic idea that she deserved to be punished. Alison immediately wanted to find out where this belief came from and started to blame her neglectful mother. However, I discouraged Alison from doing this and explained to her that no one can know for sure where our irrational ideas come from and that blaming her mother would only make matters worse. Once Alison could accept this line of thinking, I instructed her to send the loving light of her symbol to herself and her mother, and to wish her mother to be happy from the bottom of her heart. When Alison came back after two weeks, she reported that all her sadness had gone and that she had had the best conversation with her mother in years. Subsequently, Alison started to go on blind dates and continued to feel much happier than before. Her sadness and her neurotic beliefs about deserving to be punished simply disappeared.

Summary

People *who do not have any spiritual beliefs can think of their Higher Consciousness as the part of their mind that is more loving, happy and wise than they feel at the moment.*

We do *not need to have a mystical vision of our Higher Consciousness for Higher Consciousness Healing to be effective. We can simply choose how we want to perceive our Higher Power, for example, as the central figure of our religion, as a beautiful angelic being or simply as a shimmering light.*

Even *though we may use different images for our Higher Consciousness, we always share it with all beings in the universe.*

Our Higher *Consciousness is always beautiful, wise and loving. If it seems ugly, judgmental or critical, we are actually perceiving our personal consciousness.*

Chapter 9
Exploring our life-path

The next part of Higher Consciousness Healing is called 'exploring our life-path'. Before I go into this chapter, I first want to say that exploring our life-path is not essential for Higher Consciousness Healing to work. This part of the practice simply allows us to understand ourselves more deeply and receive additional feedback. Therefore, it is possible to skip this part of the practice and proceed immediately to ask for a healing-symbol as described in the next chapter.

To explore our life-path, we need to imagine our Higher Consciousness sitting on top of a mountain. As I mentioned before, we do not need to 'see' a clear picture when we visualise this. It is enough to have an idea of the mountain and of our Higher Consciousness. Then we ask our Higher Consciousness to show us a road, a path or a track leading up the mountain towards the top. This image of a path will just 'pop' into our mind and it symbolises our life-path. This path is our personal route towards our highest unfoldment.

We all lead different kinds of lives. One person is a computer consultant and another is a teacher or a housewife. Whether the life we have chosen makes us happy or not depends on one fact alone - whether it brings us nearer to our Higher Consciousness so that we can finally unite with it. In our picture, this journey is symbolised by the path that leads towards our Higher Consciousness on top of the mountain. There are as many different roads towards our Higher Consciousness as there are beings. Nobody needs to develop in exactly the same way as anybody else and we are all free to find the path that perfectly suits our needs and talents. It is not so much what we are doing that is the most important factor; what counts is our *motivation* for doing it.

Walking on our life-path and finally uniting with our Higher Consciousness means realising the love and compassion for all beings that is dormant within us. It means becoming truly and deeply happy while gaining the liberating wisdom that teaches us the true nature of the universe. It also means helping others to realise the happiness we have found for ourselves.

Different people see their life-paths in very different ways. For some, it is a wide paved road while for others, it is a steep rocky path. Most people see their life-path as having different sections representing the different phases in their life which are more or less difficult to traverse.

Once we have received an answer from our Higher Consciousness, we need to express our gratitude. Every time we acknowledge the help we receive, we become more open and receptive. And the more open we are, the more we will receive the full benefit of this work.

In what way do we receive answers from our Higher Consciousness?

Unfortunately, there is not much that distinguishes messages from our Higher Consciousness from our own thought processes. The messages may come into your mind as thoughts or images accompanied by feelings and body sensations. Even if these images and ideas feel inspiring, unfortunately, there is no guarantee that they are genuinely and exclusively channelled from our Higher Consciousness. It is important to be realistic about this in order not to fall into the trap of a spiritual 'ego-trip'. So, we need to take whatever comes into our mind with a pinch of salt and see if it makes sense to us. What matters is whether we can learn something from the images that we receive. A helpful message from our Higher Consciousness feels *good* and it is often accompanied with a sense of relief.

For most people, it is fairly simple to receive messages from their Higher Consciousness but sometimes they have a feeling that the images they receive are their own fantasy or even pure nonsense. If you feel like this, you can ask your Higher Consciousness one more time. Watch out for an inner feeling of 'yes', a feeling of relief or relaxation, or for a deep out-breath. These are all signs that you are on the right track. If you feel uncomfortable with your message, your inner image has probably come from your personal consciousness and you should go back to your relaxation and try again.

It is not a good idea to ask our Higher Consciousness the same question more than two or three times in a row because the part of our mind that receives answers on an intuitive level tires quickly. It is better to give ourselves a break after two or three attempts and try again later. With practice, our intuition will sharpen and it will become easier to receive messages from our Higher Consciousness. What is important is not to give up too soon.

Sometimes, people say that they do not get a response at all when they ask their Higher Consciousness a question. In most cases, this is not true. Many people do get an inner picture or thought but they quickly dismiss it. Unfortunately, by dismissing what came into their mind, they have shifted their state of consciousness and are less connected to their Higher Consciousness. If you find that you are not getting any answers from your Higher Consciousness, check whether you have dismissed the very first (and maybe shadowy) thought that came into your mind after you asked your question.

Exploring our problem with the imagery of the life-path
In the next step, we ask our Higher Consciousness to show us where we are on our life-path. We might receive a picture or an idea of ourselves standing way down in the valley or we might see ourselves already near the top. It really does not matter where we are on our life-path. What matters is that we are moving forward. As long as we are walking in the right direction, we will be happy no matter whether we are still in the valley or already near the top.

The first time I asked to be shown my life-path, I saw a huge mountain. It had a rocky slope near the top that only an experienced rock climber would be able to climb. In the middle, there was a steep, stony path and near the bottom was a fairly flat, wide road. I saw myself on this road down in the valley. I was pleased with this image because I liked the prospect of a flat, easy road for a while.

Our life-path represents the path of our personal and spiritual growth and it shows the shortest and the most harmonious way to develop our full potential. We are all different and what works for one person might not work for another. This is as true for learning a new language as it is for developing our personal and spiritual potential. If you see several paths leading up to the mountain top, it is always the shortest path that will bring you the deepest happiness.

We are completely free to decide whether we want to follow our life-path or not. This means that we can choose for ourselves whether or not we want to grow personally and spiritually. Nothing and no one can force us to climb up the mountain and develop our potential. Not even our Higher Consciousness can do that.

The obvious question that follows is, 'How can I make sure that I am following my life-path?'

The answer is that to move along our life-path, we need to develop a compassionate heart and a wise mind no matter what is happening to us. By contrast, if we become bitter or depressed and allow ourselves to be controlled by others, our progress on our life-path will be slow. On our life-path, there are no problems – only challenges that we are happy to overcome. On our life-path, we may experience adversity but we will know how to turn problems into wisdom and compassion. For example, if we feel rejected and harmed by others, following our life-path means developing extraordinary compassion instead of becoming resentful or depressed. If we are ill, following our life-path means finding a way to use this illness for personal growth instead of becoming full of self-pity.

But please do not think that suffering is something bad or a sign that we are failing in our development. On the contrary, for most of us, suffering is the only thing that will turn us again and again towards a concern for our inner growth. Without problems, most of us would never dream of following a path of self-development that involves effort and discipline. Only by acknowledging our suffering can we use it to progress along our life-path more happily.

Therefore, with the next question, we ask our Higher Consciousness what we are doing on our life-path when we experience our suffering from our problem. For example, we might receive images of walking slowly and with effort. We are even more likely to be shown that we are standing still, sitting down, moving backwards or even moving along other paths which lead us away from our Higher Consciousness. When we ask this question, we need to go back to our initial definition of our problem (see Chapter 5) and ask in the following way:

'Higher Consciousness, can you please show me what I am doing on my life-path when I suffer from feeling (emotion) about...?'

Here are two examples of the answers my clients received to this question
Rob suffered from money worries. When he asked his Higher Consciousness what he was doing on his life-path when he was suffering from feeling worried about his financial situation, he saw himself crouching down and feeling tense.
Claire suffered from a major problem in her relationship with her boyfriend. When she asked her Higher Consciousness what she was doing on her life-path when she felt angry with her boyfriend, she saw herself walking along a different path that led away from her Higher Consciousness.

Most people readily receive inner pictures or ideas when they ask what they are doing on their life-path when they are experiencing their problem. Also, for most people, these images make immediate sense. When we are confronted with the truth it is as if something clicks into place. Pictures are like clues and can give us a general idea of what is going on. For example, Claire with her anger about her boyfriend realised in a flash that if she carried on in the same way with her boyfriend, she would become more and more unhappy.

Again, please do not judge yourself if you find that you are not walking happily along your life-path. Instead, see this information as the first step to improving your life. After all, if we do not know that we have lost our life-path, we cannot do anything to return to it. The following list gives a rough guideline of how to interpret the imagery of the life-path. However, please feel free to interpret your life-path in the way that feels true to *you*. The following examples are intended to be guidelines and they are not hard and fast rules.

How to interpret the imagery of our life-path

There is a steep path in front of us: *The next phase of our development will be hard work but very rewarding.*

There is a flat path in front of us: *The next phase of our development will be easy.*

There is a fork in the path: *There is a possibility that lures us away from our original path.*

We can only see bits of our life-path: *We do not see our life's purpose.*

Our path disappears behind the back of the mountain: *We do not know how we want our life to unfold.*

The path seems to disappear altogether: *We feel confused and without direction.*

There is a river crossing our path: *We are experiencing big obstacles.*

There are big rocks on our path: *We are experiencing big obstacles.*

We are walking on scree: *We are experiencing many small obstacles.*

Our path is smooth: *We do not experience any obstacles.*

We see ourselves in a dark forest: *It depends what a dark forest means to us – it could mean we feel hopeless and trapped or we feel surrounded by protective forces.*

We walk through a bleak and rocky terrain: *Our life feels barren and hard.*

We walk through a beautiful landscape: *Our life feels beautiful and harmonious.*

The weather is sunny/rainy/grey: *Our emotional landscape is happy/sad/joyless.*

We are looking downhill instead of uphill: *We are looking away from the solution to our problem.*

We are standing still: *We do not actively work for the resolution of our problem.*

We are sitting down: *We feel hopeless, confused or we are lazy.*

We are walking downhill: *We are actively moving away from the solution to our problem.*

We are walking in parallel to our path through difficult terrain: *We are making it unnecessarily hard for ourselves.*

We are walking on another path away from our original path: *We have lost our life's purpose.*

We move forward but very slowly: *We are going in the right direction but we are making it unnecessarily hard for ourselves.*
We are moving back and forth: *We are undecided.*
We tread on the spot: *The way we are trying to solve our problem is fruitless.*
We move forward at a good speed: *We are solving our problem in the best way possible.*

The following case study shows how the imagery of the life-path can give us feedback on our progress.

Case study: Roger
Roger contacted me because he had lost his job and was unable to find another one. He was beside himself with anxiety. Roger was an atheist and chose to see his Higher Consciousness as a shimmering light. He was shown his life-path as a steep, rocky path and Roger saw himself halfway up the mountain in front of a torrential stream that blocked his way. When Roger asked his Higher Consciousness what he was doing on his life-path when he suffered from fear about his work situation, he saw himself walking nervously back and forth along the stream. All this made perfect sense to Roger because it mirrored his anxiety and indecision. He then received a healing-symbol – a golden star – and he worked with it for two weeks. When Roger came back to me, he reported that he felt much calmer and had been able to think more rationally about his problem. He had even started to consider new career possibilities. I guided him into relaxation and instructed him to ask his Higher Consciousness what he was doing on his life-path. To Roger's surprise, he discovered that a

bridge had appeared across the wild river and Roger saw himself walking slowly over the bridge. This image reassured Roger that he was on the 'right' path. In the following weeks and months, Roger started his own business with the help of a friend and the imagery on his life-path 'improved' simultaneously. Obviously, Roger felt a lot better as well.

This case study shows how we can check the imagery of our life-path again and again to receive feedback from our Higher Consciousness on how we are doing. In the many years that I have been working with my clients with this imagery, I am still surprised how accurate it is. Only very rarely do people receive images that do not make sense to them. If this happens to you, feel free to dismiss these images as they are not essential for Higher Consciousness Healing to work.

Summary
Working with the life-path imagery is not essential for Higher Consciousness Healing and you can skip it if you experience problems with it.
Our life-path is the path of our own personal and spiritual development and it leads towards our Higher Consciousness. It is our own choice whether we want to follow it or not.
Ask your Higher Consciousness to show you your life-path and where you are at the moment.
Messages from our Higher Consciousness come into our mind as images or thoughts accompanied by feelings or body sensations. If we are not sure whether we have received a genuine message

from our Higher Consciousness, we can ask again. Feelings of well-being and relief are signs that we are on the right track.

Ask your *Higher Consciousness: 'Can you please show me what I am doing on my life-path when I suffer from feeling (emotion) about...?'. On our life-path, there are no problems – only challenges that we are happy to overcome. Therefore, when we are suffering, it is a sign that we are straying from our life-path or standing still.*

After working *with Higher Consciousness Healing for two weeks, you can ask the life-path question again and see how the imagery has 'improved'.*

Chapter 10
Asking for a healing-symbol

Now we come to the heart of Higher Consciousness Healing practice. After we have explored our problem with the life-path questions, we can now ask for a healing-symbol to overcome our suffering. It is important to use the exact definition of our problem that we formulated earlier (see Chapter 5). Then we can ask for our healing-symbol in the following way:

'Higher Consciousness, can you please give me a healing-symbol to overcome my suffering from feeling (emotion) about...'

Someone who suffers from being depressed about not having a partner could ask in the following way: 'Dear Higher Consciousness, can you please give me a healing-symbol to overcome my suffering from feeling depressed about not having a partner.' She should not ask: 'Dear Higher Consciousness, can I please have a symbol for finding a boyfriend?' If we define a specific aim - as in the second example - we are limiting the ways in which our Higher Consciousness can solve our problem. But if we are completely open to whatever way our Higher Consciousness wants to help us, the whole process will be much more effective. As I was writing this, my friend Robert 'phoned me and told me about his latest results with Higher Consciousness Healing in solving his financial worries. His story illustrates this dynamic quite clearly.

Case study: Robert

Robert had retired early and worried a lot about money and how he could survive on his small pension as he grew older. Sometimes, these worries were so bad that he felt panic-stricken. Two months before we met, he had decided to use Higher Consciousness Healing to solve this problem. He measured his suffering from feeling anxious as seven on the scale and asked for a healing-symbol. He received a beautiful gemstone and, after working with it for two weeks, he felt a lot calmer in himself. Then something astonishing had happened. A chain of unlikely coincidences led him to the house of a friend of a friend in his favourite seaside town. They had a lovely afternoon together and chatted about many things. One topic was house prices and Robert learnt to his astonishment that house prices in this seaside town were only half as high as in the town where he lived. In a flash, he realised that this could solve all his money problems. If he sold the house he lived in, he could not only move to his favourite seaside town but he would also have plenty of money for his old age. Robert has been zero on the scale of money worries ever since.

This case study shows that Higher Consciousness Healing can bring solutions to our problems that are very unexpected and astonishing. Therefore, it is important to keep an open mind as to how our problem can be solved. If we are lucky, we may find that the solution is easier than we thought.

There is a multitude of possible healing-symbols that might pop into our mind after we have made our request to our Higher Consciousness. For a symbol to work, it needs to have a beautiful form and a bright colour. A symbol that looks ugly, boring or has a dark or dull colour cannot represent the solution to our problem. Here is a non-exhaustive list of possible healing-symbols:

Possible healing-symbols
A brightly coloured geometrical form
A piece of beautiful jewellery
Gemstones
The sun or a shining star
A brightly coloured animal
An angelic being surrounded by beautiful light
The blue sea or a green meadow
A brilliant white cloud in a radiantly blue sky
A brightly coloured flower or a bunch of flowers
A bright green tree

You need to like your symbol

It is important that you only accept a healing-symbol from your Higher Consciousness that you feel good about. If you do not like your symbol, it won't be able to enter deeply into your unconscious mind and do the transformative and necessary work. The following two case studies illustrate this point.

A client of mine suffered from depression and she received a beautiful red ruby as a healing-symbol. When she came back to me, she complained that she had not improved one little bit. When I quizzed her about the details of her process, she told me that she had initially liked her red ruby but later it reminded her of blood which she found very repulsive. Obviously, she could not recover in that way. Her next symbol was a blue sapphire that helped her to overcome her depression wonderfully.

Another client of mine had a great problem with throwing anything away so her apartment was filled with an incredible amount of stuff. She received a pink axe as a healing-symbol, which seemed appropriate at first glance. But I was suspicious because, usually, our Higher Consciousness does not give us such 'aggressive' symbols. So I asked my client how she felt about her healing-symbol and, sure enough, she said she felt ambivalent. I suggested that she ask for a more pleasant symbol and in the end, she received a pink heart - this she used successfully.

If you receive a healing-symbol that does not feel good to you for whatever reason, you need to ask your Higher Consciousness for another one. *Do not take a symbol you feel ambivalent about and do not try to change the symbol yourself.* Always ask your Higher Consciousness to give you another symbol. But one word of caution: If you have not received a good healing-symbol after three or four tries, give yourself a break and try again later. The part of your mind that can receive information on an intuitive level can tire quickly. This is especially true if we become impatient or frustrated.

Sometimes, people receive more than one symbol. If this happens, you can simply choose the symbol you like best.

The importance of a bright colour

Different colours have different healing qualities and that is why they are used to cure emotional and physical problems in different forms of colour therapy. Surprisingly, it does not seem to matter whether we experience 'real' coloured light from a lamp or whether we just imagine it. The healing-process works in either case. So when we work with Higher Consciousness Healing, we need to use a healing-symbol with a bright and beautiful colour. If our healing-symbol is white, it needs to be a very radiant and brilliant white.

In my experience, the following colours do not work: black, brown, beige, grey, all dark colours, all pastel colours and transparent symbols. If you receive a symbol with such a colour, you should simply ask your Higher Consciousness for a brighter colour or a new symbol altogether. For example, one acquaintance of mine had worked with Higher Consciousness Healing all by herself but had achieved hardly any improvement with her anxiety disorder. When I asked her about her symbol, she said she had received a transparent ring. I told her that a transparent symbol would not work and that it needed to be a strong, radiant colour. So my friend sat down again to ask for another symbol. This time she received a golden ring and her anxiety reduced greatly.

If you know a lot about colour therapy, it is best to put to one side your knowledge about which colour is meant to cure which problem when you ask for your healing-symbol. Instead, allow yourself to be surprised by the colour your Higher Consciousness shows you. What matters is that you *like* your symbol. For example, in traditional colour therapy, the colour red is an invigorating colour and blue has calming properties. However, quite a few of my 'anger clients' have successfully worked with bright red symbols. Why that is, I cannot say – I leave all this to the wisdom of our Higher Consciousness.

Troubleshooting

Once we have asked our Higher Consciousness for a healing-symbol, it will just pop into our mind as anything ranging from a clear image to a vague thought. As I have mentioned before, it is not necessary to visualise it clearly. If you have only received a vague idea about a symbol, just ask your Higher Consciousness if this is the right symbol and check for an inner feeling of confirmation. If you get an inner feeling of 'yes' (or at least not a 'no') and you really like this symbol, you can go ahead and work with it. If you cannot 'see' your symbol at all, it is best to make a simple drawing of it.

For most people, their symbol comes to them within a split second after asking their Higher Consciousness. So it is important to pay close attention in order not to miss it. Sometimes, people dismiss their first image and, afterwards, their mind seems to be blocked. To avoid this happening, try to acknowledge whatever comes into your mind. If you do not like what you see, you can simply ask for another symbol. If you have still problems receiving a symbol, here are some suggestions of what you can do:

Check *whether you have dismissed the first thought that came into your mind after asking for your healing-symbol. If this was the case, ask your Higher Consciousness if your first thought was the right healing-symbol.*
Maybe *you expected to 'see' a symbol but instead you 'heard' an idea for a symbol. Maybe you even 'felt' a symbol. Check whether you have received a symbol through a different channel from the one you expected.*

Maybe *you were not relaxed enough to receive a symbol. Go back to your relaxation and try again a little later.*

Try to *make your request for a symbol to your Higher Consciousness with more passion. Really mean it!*

Before *you ask for your healing-symbol, picture a lake. When you make your request to your Higher Consciousness, see a symbol emerging from the middle of the lake.*

Before *you ask for your healing-symbol, picture the night sky. When you make your request to your Higher Consciousness, see your symbol emerging out of the sky like a UFO.*

Before *you ask for your healing-symbol, picture a desert. When you make your request to your Higher Consciousness, see your symbol emerging like a mirage.*

Before *you ask for a healing-symbol, take a notepad and a pen. When you make your request to your Higher Consciousness, let your hand draw or write down an idea of a symbol.*

Before *you ask for your healing-symbol, imagine a radio. When you make your request to your Higher Consciousness, 'hear' a response coming from this radio.*

Before *you ask for your healing-symbol, take a medium-sized piece of clay or something similar into your hands. When you make your request to your Higher Consciousness, let your hands form a rough symbol.*

If a friend *or a therapist is guiding you through this part of Higher Consciousness Healing, they can ask your Higher Consciousness for a healing-symbol on your behalf. They should ask out loud in the following way: 'Higher Consciousness, can you please give (your name) a healing-symbol to overcome his/her suffering from feeling (emotion) about....' You need to listen to their* request and then pay close attention to any idea of a symbol that may appear in your mind.

If all else fails, let your friend or your therapist receive a healing-symbol on your behalf. Only accept a symbol that you really like.

Last but not least, thank your Higher Consciousness once you are satisfied with the symbol of your choice.

Case study: John
John came to see me because he suffered from depression. Like many of my clients, he launched into a long explanation of why and how his depression had been caused by his alcoholic mother. After empathising with John's feelings, I told John him that – despite the popularity of these ideas – there is no proof that our current problems are caused by our childhood experiences. In fact, I have found that blaming our parents makes people feel like victims and we become even more depressed. To solve his problem, I showed John how to send love to himself as well as to his mother with the help of a healing-symbol and to sincerely wish for her to be happy. At the same time, he needed to relax the tensions in his chest that were associated with his depression. In that session, John completely dissolved all his depression, which had not happened for years. It took exactly four weeks before John could do all this by himself and feel joy and optimism in all areas of his life. Simultaneously, his relationship with his mother improved as well. John told me that he could now visit her without getting angry, which, for him, was a 'mini enlightenment'.

Summary

Ask for *your healing-symbol in the following way: 'Higher Consciousness (or whatever name you call him or her), can you please give me a healing-symbol to overcome my suffering from feeling (emotion) about...'.*

If you *receive more than one symbol, you can pick the one that feels best for you.*

Your *healing-symbol must have a beautiful and bright colour.*

If you *do not like your symbol, you should ask for another one.*

Chapter 11
Working with our healing-symbol

In this chapter, I will go into some detail about how to work with our healing-symbol. Unfortunately, this may make the process appear more complicated than it is in practice. Therefore, I will first give you a short summary of how to do it:

See or sense your healing-symbol in the middle of your chest.
While you breathe out, radiate the colour of your healing-symbol throughout your body and surround yourself with a bubble of loving, joyful light.
When you breathe in just relax. Next, exhale the positive qualities of the symbol again.
If other people are involved in your problem, breathe the loving light of your symbol to them as well and see them surrounded by bubbles of loving, joyful light. Your bubble and their bubble may touch but they must not merge. Know that everyone who is genuinely happy would immediately repent their wrongdoing and become very likeable.
Relax the physical tensions that are associated with your painful emotions.

Quite a few of my clients who suffer from anxiety immediately start to worry that they are not working with their healing-symbol correctly. My advice is always the same – if it feels good, it will do you good. Working with your symbol should be an altogether pleasurable activity and at no time should it feel like a strain. Therefore, it is important not to worry that you may be doing it in the wrong way. If you get distracted, simply relax and come back to your healing-symbol.

Visualising your symbol in the middle of your chest

In the middle of our chest, beneath the breastbone, we find what I call our spiritual heart. It is from here that our deepest fulfilment and happiness arises. Our spiritual heart is the source of the love and the wisdom that we are all searching for and it is the only place where unhappiness can be transformed into happiness. Our spiritual heart is also the place where we can connect with our Higher Consciousness.

If we were able to experience our spiritual heart directly, we would find only space. This space is as wide as the universe and as bright as the sun and it is vibrant with the beautiful energy of love and joy. It is the true nature of our being and the true nature of our Higher Consciousness. This space is pregnant with all possibilities. Anything can arise from it – including the solution to our problem. Into this space, we place our healing-symbol. We do not think of our heart as a small physical organ but as limitless space vibrating with love and joy. By putting our healing-symbol into our heart, we can increasingly connect with our Higher Consciousness and gradually learn to receive the answers to all of our problems.

How does opening our heart contribute to finding happiness? Remember a time when you talked about a painful problem to someone and afterwards, you felt better. What exactly made the shift from unhappiness to happiness? Was it how you analysed the problem when you talked about it? Was it the clarity of the advice you received from the other person?

Probably not. When we are unhappy, our heart is closed and we feel better when our heart can open again because this is the only way to reconnect to unconditional happiness. This opening of the heart is most likely to happen when somebody listens to us sympathetically and appreciatively. The other person's sympathy comes directly from their heart and touches the hardened walls of our heart. If we can surrender and allow ourselves to be touched in our most vulnerable spot, the walls and knots in our heart will melt away and we will feel better again. Our emotional space can widen and fresh ideas about how to solve our problem may come to us.

Unfortunately, most of us do not have access to such a supportive listener all the time. However, Higher Consciousness Healing allows us gently to connect with our heart ourselves and activate its power to transform unhappiness into happiness. By visualising our healing-symbol in the middle of our spiritual heart, the transformation of our problem will come from the most loving and sacred place within us. Doubts, confusion and neurotic symptoms will fade away and our self-confidence will become much stronger. All our relationships will improve even if the other person does not know about our practice. In other words, an open, loving heart is part of the solution to all our problems.

Sometimes, people have difficulty in clearly visualising their healing-symbol. It can appear vague and fragmented, it can disappear, become distorted, change into another symbol or even break apart. All this does not need to be a problem. Simply return to the original symbol as it was given to you by your Higher Consciousness every time you lose it. If you have trouble visualising, you can make a simple drawing of your symbol and look at it instead of trying to visualise it.

Case study: Ruby (beginning)

The following case study stretches throughout this chapter and is the account of just one single session with Ruby. The actual work with her symbol took roughly 15 minutes. Ruby came to see me because she suffered from stress at work and, in particular, she was afraid of a colleague who had been bullying her for a long time. On top of this, Ruby beat herself up for being unable to stand up to this colleague. Ruby was in a state of great anxiety while she was with me that measured 8 out of 10 on the scale of fear (which is close to a panic attack). She received a blue flower as a healing-symbol. After working with it for 15 minutes, all her fear dissolved and Ruby was zero on the scale. However, before we even started, Ruby had trouble visualising her symbol and was very worried that she would do it all wrongly. Therefore, I reassured her that the correct visualisation was not necessary and asked her to draw a simple picture of her blue flower, which she did. (To be continued.)

Breathing out the colour of our symbol

We now let the colour of our healing-symbol radiate out throughout our body and around ourselves with each out-breath. The positive qualities of the symbol are transmitted through its colour and its particular vibration. For example, the symbol of a bright yellow sunflower can stand for joy in life and childlike innocence. All these qualities are contained in its yellow colour. So when we breathe out, we both feel and see how our body becomes filled and surrounded with loving and joyful yellow light. In this way, our whole being becomes filled with the love and the meaning of our healing-symbol. If we have a pink healing-symbol, we lovingly breathe out pink light and if we have a blue symbol, we breathe out blue light. If we have received a healing-symbol with two or more colours, we can simply choose which of the colours we want to concentrate on, we can visualise one colour after each other or visualise several colours together.

When practising Higher Consciousness Healing, we should never force or exaggerate our breath but exhale in a very relaxed and natural way. It is important always to breathe through our nose. After we have exhaled, we let the inhalation come in its own rhythm and simply relax. *We should never try to breathe in more deeply than we naturally feel like doing.* Then we breathe out again and let the healing light of our symbol radiate out once more.

In Higher Consciousness Healing, all the 'activity' always happens on the out-breath and never on the in-breath. During inhalation, we do nothing and simply relax. Only during the out-breath do we visualise how the loving light of our symbol radiates out. There is an important reason for working in this way: Breathing out makes us relaxed and breathing in makes us tense. You can try this out. Simply breathe in deeply twenty times and fill your lungs to their capacity. Most people will start to feel slightly tense and some people will even develop a bit of headache or chest pain. By comparison, after concentrating on twenty relaxed out-breaths, most people feel a lot calmer.

Unfortunately, some people have problems with all breathing exercises and they suddenly start to breathe in a strained and unnatural way. If this happens to you, please forget about the breathing part of Higher Consciousness Healing. Simply focus on your healing-symbol and send out its good qualities without connecting the process to your breath. If that works for you, it is better than creating new problems with the breathing part of the practice.

The anti-anxiety breathing technique

There is a slight variation of breathing that is helpful for all problems that fall into the anxiety category such as fear, panic and nervousness. To calm all these emotions, we need to breathe *less*. When we are afraid, we all breathe too fast and too much and this strongly contributes to all forms of fear. Once we slow down our breathing, these painful feelings quickly die down. This is how it is done:

See your *healing-symbol in your heart and breathe out its colour and good qualities with love as described before. It is most important to always breathe through your nose and never through your mouth.*
Once you *have breathed out, notice the gap before the next inhalation. Slowly start to lengthen this gap by counting slowly. Relax as much as you can while you count.*
Breathe *in again before you feel uncomfortable and immediately out again. (Never hold your in-breath when you are scared as this will strongly increase your anxiety!)*
At the *end of the out-breath, count again as far as possible while relaxing more and more deeply. (Breathe in, breathe out, one…*

two... three... four... etc... breathe in, breathe out, count... and so on.)
Carry on this breathing technique until your anxiety has disappeared. (A deeply relaxed person can have gaps of up to 20 seconds between the exhalation and inhalation.)

The anti-anxiety breathing technique is very powerful and it has brought profound relief to *every single one* of my clients suffering from fear, panic or anxiety. To do it correctly, you do not need to achieve 20-second gaps but you do need to make sure that you *never* breathe through your mouth, that you *never* breathe in more deeply than feels comfortable and that you *never* hold your in-breath.

Case study: Ruby (continued)
I asked Ruby to look at her drawing of her symbol and to let its blue colour radiate throughout her body and relax with every out-breath. After doing this for one minute, Ruby relaxed a little bit and her fear went down from 8 to 7. I then showed her the anti-anxiety breathing technique. Like most chronically fearful people, Ruby had a habit of taking fast and shallow breaths through her mouth - making her anxiety much worse. So I instructed her to breathe through her nose and to count as far as possible at the end of each out-breath. At first, Ruby could only count to three but very quickly her breathing slowed down and she could count up to eight between exhalation and inhalation. Simultaneously, her fear went down on the scale of suffering from 8 to 5. (To be continued,)

Sending love to ourselves

The core of all happiness is a feeling of love and at the core of love are well-meaning wishes. For the transformation in Higher Consciousness Healing to happen, we do not have to be dependent on someone else to love us. We can simply love ourselves. At the same time, this love for ourselves is part of the solution to our problem. No matter why we are suffering, more love is always part of the answer. Even if our problem is physical or financial, more love will help us to relax and be more content despite external problems and adversity.

Loving ourselves is something we can easily talk about but, for many of us, it is awkward to practise. For some people, it even feels wrong - as if it will make them more self-indulgent, vain or arrogant. Fortunately, this is not true because loving ourselves will make us into more loving and happy people who genuinely have something to give to others.

There is nothing strange about loving ourselves. People who have received an abundance of love throughout their childhood, love themselves like it is the most natural thing in the world. They are often not even aware that they are doing it because for them it is second nature. It is those among us who have not received an awful lot of love throughout our lives who find it most difficult to love ourselves. But we are the ones who need this love most urgently.

It is easy to love the parts of ourselves that are already perfect. But if we want to solve our problems, we need to love ourselves *with* all our weaknesses and imperfections. The next case study shows how Annie learnt to love the parts of herself that she had hated before.

Case study: Annie

Annie was struggling with the problem of being overweight. When I told her that she should breathe the colour and the good qualities of her healing-symbol into her body with love, she looked at me with barely suppressed anger and said, 'I do not love my fat – I hate it!' Luckily, she was also able to laugh about her anger and I explained to her that loving herself with all her imperfections did not mean liking her fat. It simply means sending the colour and the positive qualities of her symbol to herself like a loving gift. What counted were her good intentions for her body and that she stopped hating herself and her fat. Annie understood what I meant and she breathed the colour of her symbol into her body with the positive intention that her fat cells should transform in the most healthy and happy way. And it worked! Annie lost all the weight she wanted through some moderate changes in her diet and exercise programme.

I have used Higher Consciousness with various clients suffering from overweight, eating-disorders and alcohol addiction. They all, virtually without exception, simply stopped over-eating and drinking once they were able to send love to themselves with the help of a healing-symbol.

Love for ourselves and others is the core of Higher Consciousness Healing and it is of paramount importance to get this part of the practice right. It is much more important than breathing properly or visualising clearly. Here is a little exercise that you can use to get a loving feeling going. You can use it each time you have trouble feeling the love from your healing-symbol.

Feeling more love for yourself

Think of *someone who you find easy to like and love. This might be your child, your partner or even a pet. See this being in front of your inner eye and wish them to be happy with all your heart. Notice the warm feeling in your chest that arises when you make this wish.*

Turn your *loving intention towards yourself without changing it and wish yourself to be happy from the bottom of your heart. Love yourself **with** all your weaknesses and imperfections. Visualise the love for yourself as a beautiful light that surrounds you like a big bubble that is as wide as your outstretched arms.*

Say very *lovingly to yourself, 'I wish myself to be happy.'*

Each time *you lose this warm feeling, go back to the beginning of this exercise and remember how it feels to be loving by thinking of someone you find easy to love. Then turn this feeling of love to yourself and allow it to radiate throughout and around your whole being together with the light of your healing-symbol.*

I once had a client who suffered from terrible anger and envy because she felt that everyone had a better life than she had. As with all my other clients, I showed her how to send love to herself and these extremely painful feelings subsided each time we worked in this way. Unfortunately, whenever this woman was by herself, she only ever did Higher Consciousness Healing 'in a mechanical way'. Sadly, she was one of the very few clients who did not benefit a great deal from working with me. Therefore, it is paramount to generate a genuine feeling of love - as I described in the exercise above. To my joy, 99% of the clients with whom I have worked in the last ten years could do this after a very short time and were able to reap the full benefits of this practice.

In Higher Consciousness Healing, we imagine that joyful love emerges from the healing-symbol in our heart and fills up our entire body. The loving, joyful light then radiates beyond our body boundaries and surrounds us like a beautiful bubble. The size of this bubble is roughly as big as our outstretched arms. Being in the bubble of joyful love should feel wonderfully warm, secure and happy. Also, feeling the boundaries of our bubble will give our unconscious mind a strong message that we are totally safe and enable us to relate to others confidently and lovingly. If we feel anxious, we can reinforce this feeling of safety by repeatedly going around the firm boundaries of our bubble of love with our inner eye.

If we use Higher Consciousness Healing to remove pain and tiredness from our body, we breathe the colour of our healing-symbol mainly to the part of our body that needs healing.

Case study: Ruby (continued)
At this point, Ruby had reduced her fear from 8 to 5 on the scale of suffering by filling her body with the blue light of her symbol and using the anti-anxiety breathing technique. I then reminded Ruby that the healing light from her symbol was full of love and asked her if she could feel this love. Unfortunately, Ruby could not. Therefore, I asked her to visualise her small children in front of her inner eye and wish them to be happy with all her heart by enveloping them with bubbles of loving, joyful light. This was no problem for Ruby and she felt a very warm feeling. I then asked her to surround herself with the same loving bubble of light and

to say to herself, 'I wish myself to be happy' - just as she had with her children. Doing this was a sort of revelation for Ruby who had suffered from self-loathing virtually all her life. To her delight, she discovered that it was perfectly within her reach to stop her self-loathing and to love herself instead. After bathing in the loving light for two minutes, her fear reduced to 3 on the scale. I also asked Ruby to go around the boundaries of her bubble with her inner eye and feel the sense of safety that this induces. (To be continued.)

Sometimes, people start to feel sad when they concentrate on loving themselves and they may even end up in a state of heart-breaking self-pity. This, of course, should not happen and we need to remember that the light of our healing-symbol is always loving *and joyful*. People who tend towards sadness should never forget to practise Higher Consciousness with a smile on their face.

Sending love to others

In the next step, we send the loving light of our healing-symbol to everyone who is involved in our problem by surrounding them with bubbles of loving, joyful light, as well. Our bubbles may touch if we wish but they should never overlap or merge.

Sending love to our adversaries is extremely liberating and will heal the effects of the most terrible traumas as well as restoring peace and harmony to our existing relationships. It is the very process of giving that makes us aware that there is an inexhaustible source of joy, love and strength within us. Even better, through giving love, we genuinely dissolve all feelings of deprivation, helplessness and victimisation. Instead, we start to feel more confident, happy and strong.

In my holistic life-coaching practice, I have worked with people who had been sexually abused as children, who had been raped, violently assaulted and who were victims of domestic violence. I explained to all of them that it is not the actual trauma from the past that causes our current problems but our *current* feelings of anger, resentment and victim-mentality. All these clients, without exception, experienced dramatic improvements in their overall well-being once they let go of these negative feelings by sending love to their perpetrator with the help of a healing-symbol.

It is important to understand that sending love to someone who has harmed us does not mean forgetting what they have done or even taking away their guilt. Nor does loving our adversaries simply mean 'forgiving' them. For example, if someone has abused a child, *nobody* is in a position to forgive this terrible wrongdoing and the aggressor has to live with their guilt for the rest of their life. Sending love to our 'enemies' simply means stopping hating and resenting the people who have harmed us and, instead, wishing them to be happy. Everyone who is happy will immediately regret all their wrongdoing and transform into somebody loving and really likeable. Therefore, the most beneficial attitude towards our adversaries is to send them love and good wishes. In other words, anger, resentment and hatred tie us to our perpetrator from the past and only love sets us free to embark on a life that is entirely free from the consequences of our terrible traumas.

Sending love to others also works like a miracle in all sorts of difficult relationships. I have worked with quite a few couples on the brink of divorce, people with strained family relations and other kinds of relationship problems. All these people could either dramatically improve their relationships by working out their conflicts or they were finally able to withdraw from abusive individuals. It is important to understand that loving our 'enemies' does not mean staying close to a cruel person or simply putting up with someone's wrongdoing without asserting our needs. It is crucial to learn to keep a clear distance from abusive people and only to consider having a relationship with them once we have received a credible apology and amends. The image of the firm bubbles that surround ourselves and everybody who is involved in our problem helps us to stabilise our ego boundaries so that we can relate in healthy ways.

Sending love to someone who has harmed us seems to be against all our natural instincts. However, all wise people tell us that 'loving our enemies' is the solution to all our problems. By comparison, punching pillows and shouting angrily - as it is regretfully done in several forms of 'therapy' - will only aggravate our anger. You can try this out. For ten minutes, hit a pillow with all your might and shout angrily at everybody who has ever hurt you. You will find that you become physically exhausted after doing this but, on a mental level, your anger will quickly return – often stronger than before. Therefore, *the genuine, lasting and complete solution to overcome the effects of past traumas and problems in relationships is love.*

It is important to include our parents in our loving wishes – particularly if we feel resentment against them. In my counselling practice, I have observed that it is outright impossible to become happy and successful while we still resent our parents. This is true even if our parents have behaved in an abusive or neglectful way. The reason for this dynamic is that by hating our parents, we also hate ourselves. I like to explain this dynamic with the image of a flowerbed. We are the flower and our parents are the flowerbed from which we grow. By resenting our flowerbed, we are poisoning it and, as a result, we cannot grow to our full potential. On the other hand, if we wish our parents happiness (no matter how much wrong they have done in our upbringing) we help to create a nourishing and fertile flowerbed from which we can grow into the most beautiful and lush plants.

To send love to our adversaries, we need to imagine them one by one in front of our inner eye (as far away or as near as feels comfortable) and imagine that the loving light from our healing-symbol envelops them in a bubble of love. In our mind, we say to the person, 'I wish you to be happy.' If we feel regret or guilt towards this person, we can say, 'I am sorry for what I have done. I wish you to be happy'; or 'I am sorry it didn't work out. I wish you to be happy'. However, sending love to others does not mean only ever speaking in a sugary voice. Quite the contrary, in my life-coaching work, I have seen that this practice enables fearful people to stand up for their rights and speak with firm clarity. Ruby's case study shows this quite clearly.

Case study: Ruby (continued)

After Ruby enveloped herself in a bubble of loving, joyful light, I asked her to send love to her bullying colleague and to see him within a bubble of loving, joyful light, as well. At first, she was very reluctant. 'I want to hate and punish him,' she said with emphasis. But I explained to Ruby that it was in her own interest that her colleague was happy because he would then stop bullying her. Finally, Ruby agreed and she sent the healing light of her symbol to her colleague and imagined that it would make him into someone happy and easy to get along with. As a result of sending love, Ruby's fear decreased even further from 3 to 2 on the scale of suffering in the session. Also, a lot of resentment she had felt alongside her fear simply vanished. For the first time since working with her colleague, Ruby caught an intuitive glimpse into his psyche and realised just how unhappy this man was in himself. This insight evoked some compassion in Ruby and she felt much more confident than before. I then encouraged Ruby to send the light of her healing-symbol to her father, as well, who she resented for being too strict with her when she was a child. (To be continued.)

It is important never to let our bubbles of loving, joyful light merge or overlap as this would result in unhealthy submission and dominance. There is only one exception from this rule - our own children before the age of puberty can be visualised *within our* bubble of light. In all other cases, our bubbles may touch if we feel very fond of the other person or they can be very far away from each other if we would like to create distance from our adversary. For example, we can visualise a difficult person two miles away so that they appear as a tiny speck on the horizon.

Sometimes, our bubbles of joyful love can seem to assume a life of their own and do things that they are not supposed to. For example, they may distort, they may become very small, they may break or they may start to merge. It may also seem that we or the other person do not want to stay in the bubbles. In all these cases, we should mentally interrupt this and simply return to our healthy image of two arm-length sized bubbles of joyful love that may touch but not overlap. If we have continuing problems with people 'escaping' from their bubbles, we can even imagine that everybody is fastened with a seat belt on a seat within their bubble of love. With time and practice, our inner image will remain more stable.

Relaxing the tensions associated with our negative emotions

Many people find that their negative emotions subside a great deal simply by sending love to themselves and others with the help of their healing-symbol. However, the final letting go of negative emotions usually happens by relaxing the physical tensions that go along with them. *Every single negative feeling manifests in our physical body as tension.* Once we have identified where these tensions are (see Chapter 5: Defining our problem) and patiently relaxed them with every out-breath, we can free ourselves from a lifetime of crippling emotions within a few weeks. By learning to relax the tensions of our negative emotions, we naturally arrive at the unconditional happiness that is the natural state of our being that was there all along.

Therefore, after we have sent love to ourselves and others, we allow the light of our healing-symbol to radiate into the part of our body that holds the tensions of our negative emotions. With every out-breath, we relax these tensions just as if we are opening up a tight fist. We can help this process along by imagining that our emotional pain is like a flower bud that opens up into a beautiful flower with each exhalation.

Sometimes, we have to focus on relaxing our negative emotions over and over again because our habitual tensions may quickly return if we do not pay attention. It is important not to be discouraged by this dynamic. If we patiently relax all the physical tension of our negative emotions, we will find that our painful feelings will come back less frequently and with less strength. Eventually, they will stay away completely. In effect, doing this work is a way of retraining our body and mind to stay relaxed and happy. To my joy, virtually all my clients were able to decrease their negative emotions significantly – and if they kept at it – dissolve them completely after a few days or weeks by using this approach.

To achieve these dramatic results, we need to become aware of even the tiniest amount of emotional tension and immediately relax it before it can build up to a full-blown emotion. For example, one of my clients called her feelings of depression 'her tsunami' which implied that her depression came in waves. I told her that as soon as she felt 'a tsunami' rolling in, she should relax her eyes and the top of her head where she usually felt these negative feelings. After practising in this way for two weeks, my client was virtually symptom-free.

Sometimes, people feel their negative emotions in several parts of their body. For example, they may feel irritation in the stomach, jaw and arms. As usual, we always start with the most painful emotion. Once we have relaxed that part of our body, we move to the next strongest emotion and dissolve all tensions one after the other.

Case study: Ruby (end)
So far, Ruby had reduced her anxiety from 8 to 2 by slowing down her breathing and sending love to herself and her bullying colleague. I then asked her where in her body she felt the remaining anxiety and she said it was in her solar plexus. So I instructed Ruby to send the loving light of her healing-symbol to her solar plexus and see it opening up like a beautiful flower. It took one last minute until Ruby's anxiety was completely gone. This was a major breakthrough because Ruby had been chronically anxious for years and hardly ever experienced moments of inner peace – let alone at a time of conflict with a bullying colleague. I instructed Ruby to carry on slowing down her breathing and sending love to herself, her colleague and her father.

When Ruby returned to me two weeks later, she told me that she had sent love to her colleague and her father on a daily basis. To her joy, she felt a lot more confident and at peace with her father. To her even greater amazement, her colleague had started to be much friendlier to her. Simultaneously, Ruby's anxiety decreased to almost zero. Interestingly, Ruby suddenly had the courage to complain to her superiors and demand that this man was removed from her department. Her manager had long known that Ruby's colleague was a troublemaker and Ruby's complaint was the last piece of evidence she needed to take disciplinary action against him. Ruby's situation at work dramatically improved along with her self-esteem over the next few months.

Relaxing physical tensions can also be used to dissolve chronic tiredness. Most people think that they need more energy when they feel tired. However, this belief is incorrect. Tiredness is a state of tension that *suppresses our energy*. Therefore, instead of trying to 'build up' more energy we simply need to relax the tensions that go with the fatigue.

Case study: Ramona
Ramona was diagnosed with chronic fatigue twenty years ago and had been treated with numerous naturopathic approaches but without much success. After she had received her healing-symbol, I showed her how to look for the tensions that produced the feeling of fatigue. At first, Ramona was reluctant and insisted that her tiredness was 'everywhere'. However, once I guided her through her body, she could identify her tiredness as tensions in her temples. I then showed her how to relax these tensions with every out-breath with the help of a healing-symbol. In her mind's eye, she should see these tensions opening out like beautiful flowers over and over again. Ramona's fatigue had been particularly bad that day but after five minutes of practising Higher Consciousness Healing, it was virtually gone. To Ramona's surprise, she felt suddenly 'quite normal'.

The anti-depression smile

Smiling is beneficial for reducing all sorts of negative emotions but it is particularly important for all emotions from the sadness category such as depression, feeling low or emotional hurt. By smiling, we help to jumpstart a positive feeling that replaces our sadness and depression.

It could not be easier: We simply focus on the *joyful* quality of the light that is radiating from our healing-symbol by putting a smile on our face. We then allow this positive feeling to radiate through our being. We do not hang on to our sadness by wondering where it has gone or whether it had something important to tell us. Instead, we remember that our true being is always happy and joyful and that smiling is simply reminding us of that fact. Simultaneously, we need to identify the physical tensions that go along with our feeling of depression and patiently relax these tensions with every out-breath as described above. Most people feel depressive feelings in their head, eyes or chest area.

Working with a symbol and smiling will also stop the negative self-talk that most people who suffer from depression repeat to themselves. Instead of telling themselves that 'everything is hopeless' and that they are 'doomed to fail', they can quickly put their mind on their symbol and have a smile on their face. In this way, they can determinedly cut through all of their negative thoughts. It is not necessary to replace negative thoughts with positive thoughts because this can be very difficult and exhausting. Simply by keeping our mind on our loving healing-symbol and focusing on a relaxed and joyful smile, the depressive thoughts have nowhere to manifest. We may then find, to our surprise, that positive thoughts spontaneously enter our mind.

Case study: Harriet

Harriet suffered from life-long depression that had no particular reason and was 'free-floating'. She also had many depressive thoughts like 'I am a failure' (Harriet was successful in her career and had many friends) and 'nothing will ever change for the better' (she had overcome a serious illness and her relationship with her parents had vastly improved during the last ten years). Harriet realised that her negative thoughts were irrational but because they popped into her head frequently, she thought they were 'somehow true'. I told Harriet that she had to get firm with her negative thoughts and that the light of her symbol was like a knife that would cut through these thoughts before they could darken her emotional landscape. I also showed her how to release the tensions in her chest that went together with her depression and to smile in order to jumpstart a positive feeling.

Harriet practised in this way and she was able to reduce her depression dramatically within four weeks. As a result, she started to go to a drama group and she also joined a spiritual circle. Doing this further improved her well-being and her life-long depression was soon a thing of the past.

Bringing it all together

When we first work with a healing-symbol, it is useful to spend some time on each part of the practice (visualising the symbol, breathing correctly, visualising the bubble of loving light for ourselves, visualising the bubble of loving light for others, relaxing emotional tensions and smiling). It will quickly emerge which of these parts brings us most relief and we can then spend the most time on this aspect of Higher Consciousness Healing. For example, some people find that sending love to themselves brings most relief while others find that relaxing their negative emotion is most liberating.

You can use your own inner guidance to decide which part of the practice you want to focus on most strongly. You can simply go with what feels best. Just make sure that love is part of your approach because it is the core of Higher Consciousness Healing. With time, simply remembering your symbol will spontaneously evoke feelings of love, relaxation and joy.

Summary

See or *sense your healing-symbol in your spiritual heart in the middle of your chest.*

While *you breathe out, radiate the colour of your healing-symbol throughout your body and see yourself surrounded by a bubble of love. Love yourself - including all your weaknesses - by wishing yourself to be happy.*

When *you breathe in, just relax. Then exhale the positive qualities of the symbol again.*

If other *people are involved in your problem, envelop them within a bubble of loving, joyful light, as well. Wish the other person happiness and know that anyone who is happy would immediately repent their wrongdoing and become very likeable.*

If you *harbour resentment towards your parents, always send love to them, as well.*

If you *still feel negative emotions, relax the tensions that are associated with them.*

If you *feel anxious, combine Higher Consciousness Healing with the anti-anxiety breathing technique.*

If you *feel sad or depressed, put a smile on your face while you practise.*

Chapter 12
Working with our healing-symbol for two weeks

After we have received our healing-symbol in relaxation, we need to work with it (as described in the previous chapter) for a minimum of two minutes twice a day in formal practice and informally every time our negative feelings come up. To achieve lasting results with Higher Consciousness Healing, we have to work with our healing-symbol for at least two weeks.

Creating a regular formal practice

For our formal practice, it is best to try to find a time when we have enough peace and quiet to fully concentrate on our healing-symbol. Most people will agree that it is always possible to squeeze four minutes into their daily routine no matter how tight their schedule is. The easiest way of creating a new habit is to add it on to a habit that already exists. For example, we could practise immediately after getting up or right after we have cleaned our teeth. One of my clients always focuses on his symbol on the train to and from work. For most people, it does not work if they just 'try to remember' to work with their symbol.

To achieve lasting results with Higher Consciousness Healing, we need to work with our healing-symbol twice a day for two weeks; this makes 28 times. If we forget to do the practice for a day or two, we can simply add those days on at the end of our two weeks. For example, if on average we forget half our sessions, we should work with our symbol for four weeks instead of two. All that matters is that we do not give up altogether.

Sometimes, people work with a symbol for a few days and as soon as their problem improves, they stop. This is not advisable because often the problem will quickly return. It is important to always complete at least two weeks with each symbol. If our problem has not completely resolved within two weeks, we can carry on with the same symbol as long as we feel is necessary.

Using our symbol informally in daily life

In addition to our formal practice, it is important to use our symbol *every time* our negative self-talk or painful feelings around our problem come up. This sounds more difficult than it is. We do not need to interrupt our activities or close our eyes to practise in daily life. It is enough if our symbol flickers through our mind every now and then and if we can think vaguely of the loving, coloured light radiating through our body and beyond. We can do this while we are having a conversation, while we are reading a book or while we are working.

Many of my clients have commented on how easy and helpful it is to focus on their symbol in difficult situations instead of being overwhelmed by their negative thoughts and emotions. For example, one of my clients suffered from social phobia. So, every time she had to confront a crowd of people, she concentrated on her symbol and slowed down her breathing. Doing this took her mind right off her anxiety and cut through her old negative habit. Within four weeks, her phobia had almost disappeared and only very rarely did she need to go back to her symbol. Her example is absolutely typical.

The earlier we notice our negative feelings, the better because it is a lot easier to cut through small emotions rather than through a fully grown temper tantrum. There is no danger in suppressing our emotions with Higher Consciousness Healing. Instead, we genuinely transform and heal them by replacing them with the loving and healing light of our symbol. In that way, our problem can be positively solved.

Sometimes, people feel swamped by negative emotions and they feel that they have to focus on their symbol 'all the time'. Luckily, for most people such trying times will quickly recede with each night's sleep they have. During sleep, our symbol can move even more deeply into our unconscious mind and set things right at the root. In that way, virtually everyone finds that their negative emotions become less – abruptly or gradually – and eventually disappear altogether.

The importance of stopping negative self-talk

It is very important to notice any form of negative self-talk and to cut it through before it can develop into a painful emotion by placing our mind on our healing-symbol. To distinguish negative self-talk from healthy and constructive self-criticism, we can ask ourselves, 'Would I talk in this critical way to my most beloved friend?' If the answer is no, we should not talk to ourselves in this negative way, either. As a general rule, all depressed people suffer from negative self-talk and most anxious people do, too. They will all benefit from dropping this negative habit and sending love to themselves instead with the help of the healing-symbol.

It is not necessary to try hard to think positively. Trying hard to think positively can quickly develop into an inner battle in which the positive and negative voices fight with each other. Therefore, all we do in Higher Consciousness Healing is replace the negative thought with the positive *image* of our healing-symbol that radiates with love. By doing this, many people find that positive thoughts spontaneously arise. Obviously, these positive thoughts are there for you to experience and enjoy.

Generally speaking, the quicker we stop our negative thoughts, the quicker we will be successful. For example, instead of thinking 'oh, my legs are so ugly' we just think, 'oh, my legs...' and before this nasty thought has finished, we quickly put our mind on our healing-symbol before it has developed into a painful emotion. Doing this is not really hard but I do admit that sometimes it can feel a bit tedious. It is just as tedious as it is to clean up our kitchen day in, day out. The good news is that our 'inner' cleaning activities will become fewer and fewer the more we focus on our healing-symbol instead of sliding back into our old emotional habits. It is absolutely possible to retrain our mind and after only a few days or weeks, our negative inner voices will give up.

Generally speaking, we cannot overdo Higher Consciousness Healing. Even if we focused on our healing-symbol all day long, it can only be beneficial and would not have any negative side effects.

Case study: Ruby
Ruby (who you met in the previous chapter) had a massive habit of negative self-talk. She had been born and raised in a country

that sees women as subordinate and she had lived through an arranged marriage with a violent man. Every day, she called herself things like 'stupid cow' and blamed herself for every little thing that went wrong around her even if it had nothing to do with her. When I told Ruby that this negative self-talk was the first thing that had to stop, she was surprised and confused. It never had occurred to her that she was harming herself by talking to herself in that negative way. However, she made a strong effort to cut through this very bad habit by placing her mind on her healing-symbol each time a self-reproach came up and quickly became better at it. After only two months, she had completely stopped calling herself names and, instead, was able to send a strong feeling of love to herself. At first, Ruby felt slightly sad that she had unnecessarily made her life such a misery with her negative self-talk but this sadness quickly disappeared. To Ruby's surprise, she suddenly had much more energy and she used this new-found energy to train for a marathon. She also joined a spiritual community where she hoped to find a new partner – this time chosen by herself.

Do not change the symbol

In the rare cases where one of my clients reported back to me that their symbol had not worked, it often turned out that they had allowed their healing-symbol to change or that they had changed it themselves. The following case study illustrates this point:

Case study: Mary

Mary had been working on her problem of depression quite successfully. When we first met, she was 7 on the scale of suffering. After four weeks of Higher Consciousness Healing, her suffering was down to 1. However, when she came to our next session, she felt dreadful again. When I asked her what had happened, she told me that she had felt that her healing-symbol had gradually 'lost its power'. She had not felt excited by it anymore and she had found it harder and harder to visualise it in its original form (a happy person standing on top of a mountain). The symbol seemed to be changing and looked more like a lonely woman in the rain. Mary had just been going along with this process and was visualising the symbol in its new and negative form. Unsurprisingly, she was feeling worse and worse. I explained to Mary that practising her new and more negative symbol would increase her inner negativity. Luckily, after realising her error, Mary returned to her original symbol and soon felt better again.

We must never allow our healing-symbol to change and we must never change it ourselves. Every time our symbol seems to change its form or colour, we need to return immediately to our original healing-symbol as it was given to us by our Higher Consciousness. It does not matter how often we have to repeat this process because it will not weaken the positive effects of Higher Consciousness Healing.

We need to work actively for a solution to our problem

While we use our symbol, we need to work actively for the solution to our problem and do everything that common sense dictates. It is no good to sit back and do nothing while hoping that our Higher Consciousness will solve all our problems. Unfortunately, it just does not work that way. The following story exemplifies this point:

A big flood had engulfed the country and Nasreddin sat on top of a tree, well above the water. Nasreddin was a very religious man. He fervently prayed to God to save him and he felt total faith in his heart that this would happen. Suddenly a boat appeared and the people in it offered to pick Nasreddin up. But Nasreddin declined and told them that he was sure that God would save him. The people in the boat tried to convince Nasreddin to join them but, finally, they gave up and went away. Another boat appeared but Nasreddin declined again. The water rose and rose and finally Nasreddin had to let go of the tree and swim in the water. Again, he prayed to God to save him and he still felt optimistic that this would happen. A helicopter appeared but Nasreddin once again declined to be picked up. As before, he told the people that God would save him. Nasreddin swam for three days and three nights in the water. Then his strength failed him and he drowned.

When he appeared in heaven in front of God's throne, he was furious. 'I prayed to you to save me,' he said angrily, 'but you let me drown! Didn't you hear my prayers?'

'I heard your first prayer,' God said mildly, 'and I sent you a boat. But you declined its help. Then I heard your second prayer and I sent another boat but you declined that one's help, as well. I also heard your third prayer and that time I sent you a helicopter but again you declined its help. What else, Nasreddin, could I have done for you?'

This story encourages us to use our common sense and use every source of help that is available to us. Sometimes, Higher Consciousness Healing will support us in doing the most obvious thing: the one that was always in front of our nose. Sometimes, we may even be lucky enough to experience a small miracle. Therefore, we should always be active and try to improve our situation in whatever way we can think of.

For those of us who find it difficult to get up and do something about our problems, here is another piece of good news. I have observed that people who previously just put up with their problems passively, suddenly become active in finding solutions when they start practising Higher Consciousness Healing. Their healing-symbol seems to remove the block that had hindered them from being disciplined and actively solving their problem.

Higher Consciousness Healing sometimes attracts other forms of help

Higher Consciousness Healing is not an exclusive method. It can work like a catalyst and trigger other processes that will help us to solve our problem. For example, sometimes, people 'coincidentally' find a book that will give them some much-needed insights or they might 'coincidentally' meet a person who can help them. The following case study demonstrates this dynamic in quite a dramatic way.

Case study: Brenda
Brenda suffered from a very painful disorder of her spine that was so disabling that she couldn't go to work and she lived on state benefits. When she talked to me, she felt so depressed that she was suicidal. I immediately helped her to receive a symbol to dissolve her despair. I only heard from Brenda two months later and she told me an astounding and unlikely story. Brenda had long been convinced that she would get optimal treatment in a special hospital in another country but she had never had the financial means to go there. After starting to work with her symbol, Brenda's depression lifted and she wrote to an airline to ask for a free ticket which she promptly received. So she flew to the other country and simply turned up at the hospital to ask for treatment. To her joy, she received treatment worth many thousands of dollars and was allowed to pay it back in small instalments. Her condition dramatically improved and she returned home with new hope. Brenda put all these unlikely coincidences down to her practice of Higher Consciousness Healing. Obviously, I cannot say if this is so. All I can say is that I have witnessed many small and larger 'miracles' when people start to connect with their Higher Consciousness and send love to their problems.

Some misconceptions about how to overcome emotional problems

Sometimes, people believe that to overcome their problems all they need is one amazing breakthrough in which everything becomes clear and then their problem will be solved once and for all. In my experience, it does not work like this. The human mind seems to need time and frequent reminders to make lasting changes.

Many problems are nothing other than habits of negative thinking and negative feelings. To overcome them, we need to let them go and replace them with positive, rational beliefs and more joyful feelings. This might sound terribly simplistic but when it comes to changing the human mind, it boils down to just that. Even if we have deep insights and amazing liberating experiences, the resulting positive emotions will often be short-lived if we do not know how to ingrain these changes into our mind. Repeating our symbol twice a day for two weeks is a means of achieving just this.

Some people try to change their negative habits of thinking and feeling just with their will-power. This usually does not work because this approach does not take into account that an unconscious part of ourselves wants to hold on to our problem. My client Paul was a good example of this.

Case study: Paul
Paul had problems with commitment in his relationships with women and had just left his wife. He had moved in with his girlfriend but they were arguing a lot because she wanted more commitment than he was willing to give. Paul had spent much of

his adult life under the influence of drugs and alcohol and had only made a half-hearted commitment to stop this. He was pretty depressed about his whole situation but he was motivated to bring about some change. His favourite approach was to use affirmations. He used to say positive statements to himself and if he felt he was resisting them, he simply repeated them to himself as often as possible. Unfortunately, the use of positive affirmations like 'I am fully alive and happy' or 'I now commit joyfully' did not help him. On the contrary, they usually made him feel worse. The more he tried to talk himself into these affirmations, the more the impulse not to commit surfaced and the more a voice in his head told him that his life was meaningless. But Paul was undeterred and struggled on repeating his positive sentences in the hope that one day he would break through his resistance.

However, once Paul used symbols, his situation improved. After several days of sending love to his wife and his girlfriend, he did what he had avoided doing all his life and what he feared most of all. He talked openly to his wife and to his girlfriend and started to relate to them more honestly. This was a major breakthrough for Paul because, throughout his adult life, he had never related to anybody in an honest way. His relationships had always been riddled with lies and dishonesty. For him to have the courage to talk to somebody honestly was like experiencing a mini-enlightenment. His depression lifted considerably and by the time he stopped coming to see me, he was about to move out of his girlfriend's flat. It had become clear to him that he was at a stage in his life where he didn't want to commit and that it was in the best interest of everybody that he lived on his own for a while.

Some people believe that it is possible to 'let feelings out' in order to get rid of them by screaming and hitting pillows. Unfortunately, the opposite is true. People who express their negative emotions *frequently* and *powerfully* will discover that their emotions increase and become harder and harder to control. The whole idea that negative emotions can somehow be expelled from our body is completely wrong. Emotions are not 'things' that can be moved from one place to another but they are mental experiences that can easily become destructive habits. The sublime pacifier of all negative emotions is love for ourselves and for others. Higher Consciousness Healing enables us to *heal* our negative emotions with love and without suppressing them.

Another destructive attitude that keeps people from finding happiness is blaming others. Unfortunately, in our society, it is still a widely held belief that our childhood experiences or other traumas from our past are somehow to blame for our present problems. I always explain to my clients that there is no proof for these theories even if millions of people believe in them. But one thing is absolutely certain – blaming others leads to victim mentality, chronic resentment and depression. Higher Consciousness Healing offers a radical and extremely quick way to overcome all real and imagined consequences from past traumas - this is to send love to the very people who have hurt us. In this way, victim mentality is replaced with confidence, resentment is replaced with inner peace and depression can easily be transformed into joie de vivre. The following case study illustrates this point quite clearly.

Case study: Karen

Karen contacted me because nothing in her life was as she wished it to be. She had no boyfriend, she didn't like her work and she thought it was impossible to get a visa for the country she wanted to live in. Karen was consumed by envy that 'everybody had what they wanted' and that she was 'irreparably scarred' by her upbringing. However, Karen freely admitted that her parents had been quite loving and I didn't see any other major trauma in Karen's life that could account for all her misery. But Karen was adamant that it was something in her childhood that had to be blamed for all her problems. After searching high and low, she finally concluded that it had to be the fact that she was a single child. She had subscribed to a website that encouraged her in this thrust of thought and was full of self-pity when she contacted me. She was quite taken aback when I (gently) disagreed with her belief system. Fortunately, after working first with one symbol about her chronic resentment and then with another about her envy, she felt so much better that she confessed to me that 'all this whining' on the single child website was really getting on her nerves. Several months later, she contacted me with the positive news that she felt strongly inspired to become a counsellor herself and – even better – this would allow her to get a student visa so she could live and study in the country of her dreams. Her whole attitude had changed from being a resentful, envious and depressed person to someone who was responsible, positive and in control.

Summary

Work with *your healing-symbol for two minutes twice a day for two weeks in formal practice.*

Determinedly *stop all negative self-talk by placing your mind on your healing-symbol as soon as a negative thought arises.*

Never allow *your healing-symbol to change of its own accord and never change it yourself.*

Actively work for the solution of your problem as common sense dictates.

Avoid *misconceptions about how to solve emotional problems such as using too much willpower, forcefully expressing negative emotions or blaming others.*

Chapter 13
Getting feedback on our process

After the first two weeks of Higher Consciousness Healing are finished, most people will experience a significant improvement in their suffering. There are two ways in which we can get feedback on our progress.

Getting feedback by asking the scale question

To get feedback on our progress with Higher Consciousness Healing, we can ask ourselves where we are on the scale of suffering (taking an average of the last three days) and then to compare this number with the one from two weeks ago. To get a correct reading, it is important to go back to the precise definition of our problem and only measure the negative emotion that we have been working with. For example, if we defined our problem as 'suffering from feeling afraid of the arguments with my partner' and we measured our fear as 8 on the scale, we should now look at how much our *fear* has decreased and not how many arguments we had or if we feel any other negative emotions.

In many cases, people have quite dramatic improvements. They might measure their suffering the first time as 7 or 8 and after two weeks, they might be down to 2 or 3. But even if we do not get this major improvement, it is good to appreciate any improvement we have achieved. In this way, we increase our confidence and determination to carry on.

Very rarely, people may have the experience that their initial negative emotion has been replaced with another negative emotion. For example, they may find that they are not afraid anymore but feel quite annoyed, instead. This may seem frustrating but it is actually a positive development. It simply means that we have worked through the first layer of our emotions and we can now work (with a different symbol) on the next layer. There is a maximum of just three layers (anxiety, sadness and anger) and most people experience only one sort of negative emotion per problem. In the next chapter, I will say more about how to work through complex problems.

It is a good idea to write down all your scale numbers in order not to miss any positive improvements.

Getting feedback by asking the life-path question

The second way to get feedback on our process is to ask our Higher Consciousness to show us our progress on our life-path. This is a more intuitive approach compared with the scale question and, as I have said before, it is not essential for Higher Consciousness Healing to work. So, if the imagery of the life-path does not appeal to you, you can leave it out altogether.

Before we can ask the life-path question, we need to recall where we were on our life-path and what we were doing two weeks earlier. If we have made progress with our problem, our Higher Consciousness should show us that we are moving forward with more confidence, (for example, walking upwards instead of standing still) and we might even find that we are a bit further up on our life-path. To ask the life-path question, we need to relax. We can then ask our Higher Consciousness:

Higher Consciousness, can you please show me what I am doing now on my life-path?

As before, watch out for the very first thought or image that pops up in your head. For most people, the imagery of the life-path is quite self-explanatory. Here is a list of what would indicate a positive improvement. For more explanations about the life-path, please return to Chapter 9.

Signs that our life-path imagery indicates an improvement
Our life*-path is more visible than before.*
We have *turned towards our Higher Consciousness.*
We are *now on our life-path instead of next to it or on other paths.*
We are *standing up instead of sitting down.*
We are *moving in the right direction.*
We have *increased our speed.*
The obstacles *on our path (rocks, streams, etc.) have become smaller, have disappeared or we have found a way around them.*
The weather *is better.*
We feel *better while we are walking*

Here are some examples of how my clients' life-path imagery changed in the process of practising Higher Consciousness Healing.

Life-path imagery at the beginning	Life-path imagery after two weeks	Life-path imagery after four weeks
Being halfway up the mountain	Being a few metres higher up	Being even higher up

Sitting down and looking down into the valley	Still sitting but looking up to the Higher Consciousness	Starting to walk toward the Higher Consciousness
A big rock obstructs the life-path	The rock has disintegrated into smaller rocks	The path is clear

The importance of appreciating our improvement

Getting feedback on our process is important for two reasons. Firstly, it serves as an encouragement and helps us to keep going. Secondly – and this is even more crucial – receiving positive feedback allows us to appreciate our effort. Doing this is extremely important because each time we consciously appreciate our ability to solve our problems, we become more confident, more able and more in control. In this way, we benefit doubly from Higher Consciousness Healing – we get rid of our problem *and* we gain the confidence to solve all our future challenges, as well.

Unfortunately, I have seen people achieve dramatic results with Higher Consciousness Healing but because they were not able to appreciate these improvements, it didn't serve them as an overall confidence boost. Even more sadly, these people quickly forgot about the method and felt as helpless as before.

Case study: Gary

Gary suffered from feeling exhausted and tired. When he asked for his life-path imagery, he saw himself lying on his life-path and sleeping. I asked Gary where in his body he felt his tiredness and after much searching, he realised that he felt tensions in his head. After he had received his healing-symbol, I showed him how to release and relax these tensions with every out-breath by imagining a beautiful flower opening up in his head.

Unfortunately, Gary's progress was slow because he always thought that the reasons for his tiredness came from outside his mind (hard work, a virus, etc.) and that he would be unable to do something himself about it. Unsurprisingly, after two weeks, he saw himself still lying on his life-path but luckily at least his eyes were half-open. This coincided with Gary feeling a little bit less tired (from 7 to 5 on the scale). I explained to Gary that our Higher Consciousness has so much energy that it could light up half of the universe for a week. The solution to his fatigue would be to let the light of his Higher Consciousness release the energy in his body that had been there all along.

Gary could accept my line of thinking and concentrated strongly to intercept even the tiniest amount of tiredness from creeping in by immediately relaxing the tensions in his head. Slowly, his condition improved as did the imagery on his life-path. After two months, he was finally standing up and after three months, he was energetically walking up the mountain. His chronic tiredness had completely disappeared despite working even harder than before.

Summary

After two *weeks, measure your amount of negative emotion on the scale (take an average of the last three days) and compare the number with the one you had two weeks earlier.*

Ask your *Higher Consciousness for your current life-path imagery and compare it with the one you received two weeks earlier. Ask in the following way: 'Higher Consciousness, can you please show me what I am doing now on my life-path?'*

Your life*-path imagery will improve according to how you have improved with your problem.*

Try to *appreciate sincerely even the smallest improvements.*

Chapter 14
Working through complex problems

If we want to address a complex problem and we know in advance that it has several aspects and layers (like the suffering arising from a divorce, for example), we should always work first with the negative emotion that causes us most suffering. For example, we can ask ourselves, 'Do I feel mostly angry, mostly sad or mostly afraid? As I have pointed out before, it is important to avoid psycho-analysing ourselves to find 'deeper aspects' or 'unconscious motivations'. It is much more important to clearly pinpoint our most painful emotion and then dissolve it by using a healing-symbol.

Once our initial negative emotion has been substantially reduced (after two or four weeks, for example), we may sometimes find that another negative emotion has come to the foreground. This is a very good sign of progress and we can simply ask for another healing-symbol to overcome this new aspect of our problem. There are only three main negative emotions: anger, sadness and anxiety (see Chapter 5) and therefore we can be assured that there will be *no* endless succession of negative feelings awaiting us. For example, in the case of divorce, there might first be a layer of despair (sadness group), then anger (at ourselves or our partner) and finally anxiety about loneliness. All these emotions can be dissolved or at least substantially reduced with Higher Consciousness Healing. The case study of Anne illustrates how to do this:

Case study: Anne

Anne worked with Higher Consciousness Healing to recover from the devastating results of her recent separation from her husband. When she came to see me, she was in emotional turmoil. Anne's husband had left her for another woman and it had come as a complete shock to her. She felt anger, grief, longing, sadness, loneliness and she was also suffering from insomnia. In our first session, I asked Anne which of all these feelings was giving her the most suffering. Unfortunately, Anne was so upset that she didn't find this question easy to answer. After talking for a while to clarify her feelings, she asked for a healing-symbol to overcome her suffering from feeling despair about her divorce. She received a golden broach as her healing-symbol. On her life-path, she saw herself halfway up the mountain, crouching down with her head down and holding herself around the knees.

Anne cried a lot during her first two weeks of Higher Consciousness Healing but she felt a genuine process of letting go. She still had waves of despair but when she remembered her healing-symbol, she got over these difficult emotions more quickly than before. After two weeks, Anne felt a bit better but still quite far away from being happy. When she looked at her life-path, she was still crouching down but she had stopped holding herself was now looking up at her Higher Consciousness. It wasn't a great improvement but this imagery served as a big encouragement to Anne.

I then asked her what was causing her the biggest suffering out of all her remaining symptoms. She said that although she felt less sad and despairing, she felt terrified at the prospect of living on her own. So this time she asked for a healing-symbol to overcome her suffering from feeling frightened of living on her own. She worked painstakingly with her new symbol for another two weeks and her fear diminished considerably. She also started meeting up with a relative and this was a great comfort to her. When she looked at her life-path two weeks later, she was standing up and had made some tentative steps up the mountain. This improved imagery served Anne once again as an encouragement.

Then I asked Anne again to find out which of her remaining symptoms was causing her the most suffering. After thinking for a while, she said that the emotional hurt of being alone (sadness group) was now the worst for her. After another two weeks, Anne felt a lot more confident and on her life-path, she saw that she had made even more steps up the mountain. Once again, Anne selected the emotion that was causing her the biggest suffering. Now she asked for a symbol to overcome her suffering from being incredibly angry about the behaviour of her husband.

At the end of these eight weeks of Higher Consciousness Healing, Anne felt much better. Her suffering from her divorce had been 8 on the scale when she had first come to see me but at the end of the eight weeks, she was down to 2 on average. Her emotional state still fluctuated sometimes but, all in all, she was over the worst.

Just as Anne did, we should always work with the negative emotion that is causing us the most suffering in a very obvious way.

Every negative emotion needs a new symbol

Every new problem and every new negative emotion needs a different healing-symbol from our Higher Consciousness and we should work with each symbol for a minimum of two weeks. After the first two weeks are up, we can continue with the same symbol for as long as we feel it is helpful. Alternatively, we can ask for another symbol for another painful emotion.

What to do in the case of relapse

With Higher Consciousness Healing, our problem will either get better gradually over time or suddenly resolve from one day to the next. But one thing is sure – our problem will return every now and then. Until our new healthy pattern is deeply established, our old negative habit is bound to come back. This is particularly true when we have had a chronic problem.

But – and this is the good news – the periods when our problem returns will get shorter and the intervals between these periods will get longer. If we know that there is a certain up and down pattern to be expected, we will feel less frustrated when our problem comes back. Whenever a symptom returns, we simply have to remember our healing-symbol and work with it until our relapse is over. We can do that in parallel with any other symbol that we may be working with at that moment.

Summary

If you have a complex problem, always start by asking for a healing-symbol for the negative emotion that is bothering you the most.

After you have finished your first two-week period of Higher Consciousness Healing, you can continue with the same symbol as long as you feel it is helpful.

Alternatively, you can ask for a new healing-symbol for a different problem and work with it for another two weeks.

Every new problem and every negative emotion needs a new healing-symbol.

If you have a relapse, simply go back to your initial symbol and work with it until the relapse is over.

Chapter 15
Using Higher Consciousness Healing for making decisions

It is possible to use the imagery of the life-path to help us make decisions. The following case study demonstrates how this can be done.

Case study: David

One client of mine, David, wanted to change his career and he was contemplating three different options. The first option was starting his own business, the second option was going back to his old teaching job and the third option was to train as a counsellor. After discussing the pros and cons of these options with David, I asked him whether he would like to consult his Higher Consciousness about it.

*David agreed and after he had relaxed, he asked his Higher Consciousness to show him his life-path and the place where he was at the moment. He saw himself a third of the way up the mountain on a narrow and steep track walking up steadily. Then David asked **what he would be doing** on his life-path if he started his own business. Immediately, he saw himself moving hectically up and down his life-path. David felt that these hectic movements symbolised the stress he would be under if he started a business and that he wouldn't make any real progress in moving closer to his Higher Consciousness.*

Then David asked his Higher Consciousness what he would be doing on his life-path if he went back to his old teaching job. Immediately, he got a picture of himself sliding down the mountainside. This answer was clear, too – if he went back to his old job, he would go backwards rather than forwards. All this made perfect sense to David. His third career option was counselling. When he asked his Higher Consciousness about this, he saw himself walking up his life-path but it seemed a rather strenuous climb. This option seemed to be more in harmony with his life-path but David felt that he wanted a less strenuous job.

I encouraged David not to trust these images blindly but to check if they made sense from a common-sense point of view. David explained that they made a great deal of sense to him and that they had shown him that none of his three career options was ideal at the moment. He decided to not change his career until he had found the type of work that would satisfy him more. He left the session with a good feeling.

With the life-path questions, we can test whether any area of our life is in harmony with our Higher Consciousness or not. Here is a list of questions we can ask:

"Higher Consciousness,...
what am *I doing on my life-path when I do a certain job?*
what am *I doing on my life-path when I am in a certain relationship?*
what am *I doing on my life-path when I pursue a certain hobby?*
what am *I doing on my life-path when I follow a particular spiritual direction or teacher?*
what am *I doing on my life-path when I am in a certain kind of therapy?*
what am *I doing on my life-path when I relate to others in a certain way?*

what am *I doing on my life-path when I pursue a certain wish?*
what am *I doing on my life-path when I move to a certain town/area/house?*
what am *I doing on my life-path when I spend my days in a certain way?"*

Of course, this list is not exhaustive and you can add whatever questions are relevant to your life. It is important to understand that we mustn't take the answers we receive to these questions as unshakable truth. Higher Consciousness Healing offers us the possibility to improve our intuitive inner wisdom but we need to be aware that in the beginning there is the possibility of error. Therefore, we should always use all our intelligence and common sense to check if our inner images make sense. Generally speaking, if we make it a habit to use the life-path imagery frequently, we are likely to develop a new and wonderful certainty about what is good for us.

Sometimes, people are a bit shocked when they discover that what they are doing does not seem to be in harmony with their life-path. But if we discover that we have made a mistake, we should not feel depressed. On the contrary, we should celebrate our discovery. Only through recognising our errors will we be able to take the appropriate steps that will enable us to develop towards more happiness and fulfilment.

Case study: Karen
My client Karen had decided to find out whether any of her relationships were out of alignment with her Higher Consciousness by checking her life-path imagery. It shocked her

a bit to discover that one of her closest friendships was actually causing her to go backwards on her life-path.

Karen thought about this picture carefully and finally admitted to herself that she had felt more and more uncomfortable with this friendship for the past two years. She realised that she had tried to ignore these negative feelings because she was quite attached to her friend. Karen was confronted through her life-path imagery with a truth she had successfully blocked out. However, once she was over her initial shock, she knew that the answer from her Higher Consciousness was right. Therefore, she decided to ask for a healing-symbol to overcome her suffering from feeling irritation in the relationship with her friend. Through this practice, Karen gained more inner distance and felt much better. She still loved her friend but she didn't feel as unhealthily attached to her as before.

Summary
You can use the life-path imagery to receive intuitive guidance to make decisions and to check if any area of your life is out of alignment with your Higher Consciousness.
Do not trust any intuitive messages blindly but use all your intelligence and common sense to check if they make sense.

Chapter 16
Maintaining well-being in every area of our life

There is a lot more we can do with Higher Consciousness Healing to help us live a happy and contented life. Besides our major personal problems, we all experience little irritations as well, like occasional tiredness, stress or performance anxiety. We all suffer from time to time from these issues because they are an unavoidable by-product of being human. Luckily, with Higher Consciousness Healing, we can do something about most of these small problems without any great effort. The following case study shows how my friend Robert used Higher Consciousness Healing for a very small problem.

Case study: Robert
My friend Robert was offered a lift to a party. He was pleased with this because it meant that he could have a drink. On the other hand, he knew that sitting in the backseat of a car always made him feel sick. Robert is an enthusiastic user of Higher Consciousness and, at once, he asked for a healing-symbol to overcome his suffering from feeling sick in the backseat of cars. He didn't even relax when asking for his healing-symbol but just asked for it shortly before he went out. He said it made a big difference and was very happy with one more success in his 'self-therapy'.

Standard-symbols

The following list shows issues that many people experience from time to time in a mild way. If any of these problems bother you in a small way, you can ask for a healing-symbol for it and only use it at the times when you experience this negative state of mind. These symbols are called standard-symbols and we do not need to work with them for two weeks.

Tiredness
Stress
Physical pain
Nervousness or mild anxiety
Small irritations and fears in relationships
Feeling uninspired and dull

My own standard-symbols are a golden hand for pain and a sparkling candle for tiredness. It is really great to have these little helps at hand when I need them. It makes the unavoidable ups and downs of life more like plain sailing.

Using the bubbles of joyful love for everyday tensions in relationships

While going about our daily activities, most people experience some awkward situations with others - tensions arising in everyday conversations or other small disruptions in their interactions with the people around them. In all these cases, we can simply visualise (or think of) the inner image of two bubbles of loving, joyful light surrounding ourselves and the other person. These two bubbles may touch but should never overlap or merge. While you are talking, you can go along the boundaries of your bubble in your mind, which will make you feel much more secure and in control. In many cases, the effects of this short visualisation are immediate and tangible. The tricky moment of the conversation is likely to pass without causing an argument, the embarrassment may subside or the feeling of being dominated will disappear. We can work in exactly the same way if we feel tormented by compulsive thinking about difficult interactions with others.

If our problem with the other person persists despite this short visualisation, we can ask for a healing-symbol and practise in a more concentrated way for a two-week period.

Clearing and harmonising our chakras

According to Tibetan Buddhism, we have 72,000 energy channels in our body and five main energy centres which are called chakras. These chakras are located in our lower abdomen, in our solar plexus, in our heart, in our throat and in our brain. With every thought we think, with every feeling we feel and with every physical movement we make, energy moves through our energy channels and through our chakras. If we have an emotional or physical problem, we will find that we have a disharmony in one of our chakras as well.

One way of maintaining our overall well-being is to create harmony in our energy system because it will, in turn, harmonise our mind, body and emotions. Many people who want to work with their energy system do this with practices like T'ai Chi, chakra meditation or Yoga. Higher Consciousness Healing offers another way of clearing, balancing and harmonising our main energy centres, the chakras.

If we feel a specific problem around one of our chakras like a lump in our throat or tension in our chest, we can ask for a healing-symbol to overcome our suffering from this blockage in the usual way. But here comes something new: healing-symbols to harmonise the chakras are not all visualised in the heart but *in the specific chakra* we are working with. If, for example, we want to work on a block in our throat chakra, we visualise our healing-symbol in our throat. We let the light of our healing-symbol expand from our throat and fill our body, our aura and our whole environment. If we are working on the navel-chakra, we visualise our healing-symbol in our navel and let the light expand from there. We should work with these healing-symbols in the usual way for two minutes, twice a day for two weeks.

Case study: Katie
Katie often suffered from an uncomfortable lump in her throat accompanied by feelings of anxiety. Her healing-symbol was shown to her as a bright, golden sun. She visualised this golden sun in her throat and expanded its light all through her body and beyond. After practising for a few days, she felt the lump in her throat melt and the feelings of anxiety decrease. She recognised that she always felt this lump whenever she feared that she couldn't connect with other people in the way she wanted. Katy found these insights interesting and carried on practising her healing-symbol. She often found that the mere thought of her healing-symbol was enough to stop the lump in her throat returning. Simultaneously, her ability to relate to others improved, as well.

Summary

You can *work on very small issues like occasional pain, stress or tiredness with standard symbols. You just use these symbols when your problem becomes acute.*

You can *alleviate occasional tensions in contact with others by visualising a bubble of love around each of you.*

Higher *Consciousness Healing can be used to clear away blocks and disharmonies in your chakras. Ask in the usual way for a healing-symbol but visualise your symbol **in the chakra** you are working with. Let its light and colour expand from there.*

Chapter 17
The ultimate healing-symbol

You might already have guessed it – the ultimate healing-symbol is our Higher Consciousness itself. We should always visualise our Higher Consciousness in a pleasing form and in very beautiful, radiant colours.

We can use this symbol in exactly the same way as we use our other healing-symbols. We visualise our Higher Consciousness in our heart and breathe its good qualities and colour to ourselves and envelop ourselves with a bubble of love. Then we breathe the loving light from our Higher Consciousness to others (our loved ones, as well as those we find particularly difficult at the moment) and envelop them with bubbles of love, as well. If you start and end your days with this simple visualisation, you will find that your life becomes happier and more successful and that obstacles will disappear more readily.

Using the symbol of our Higher Consciousness for our spiritual growth

Working with the symbol of our Higher Consciousness will help us with a kind of suffering that no kind of psychotherapy will be able to alleviate. It is the suffering that stems from the fact that we are separated from our Higher Consciousness. Even if we live in the best of all circumstances – with a fantastic career, the best of all partners, as much money as we want and whatever else is important to us – in the back of our mind, we know that we will lose all this one day. Our family might die today in a car accident and tomorrow we might be sacked from our job. No matter how hard we try to ignore this insight, there is no real security to be found in this world.

Another problem that we share with almost every human being is that nothing can completely satisfy us for long. Even if our deepest wishes are fulfilled, it is unlikely that the thrill of this fulfilment will last longer than a few months. After that time, we become used to our new situation and our deep-seated dissatisfaction will resurface and ask for 'more' and 'better'.

Most of us are not fully aware of these kinds of problems because we are so used to them. But if we do not realise that we are suffering from this 'spiritual illness', we tend to project our inner restlessness and deep-seated anxiety on to our partners, on to our jobs or on to our other life-circumstances. We just do not realise that no human condition can give us what we long for most deeply and most intensely – the recognition that we already possess the infinite love, happiness and wisdom of our Higher Consciousness. Working with the symbol of our Higher Consciousness will bring us nearer to realising this truth.

Case study: Amanda

Amanda had successfully used Higher Consciousness Healing to dissolve her chronic tiredness and her anxieties around money. However, she still experienced what she called 'mental fog' that led to confusion and unconscious acts of passive aggression. This was a very stubborn problem that Amanda had had virtually all her adult life. At the time, Amanda browsed through many different images of deities on the internet. At some point, she found an image of the Chinese goddess of compassion, Kwan Yin, that inspired her greatly. She immediately decided to visualise her Higher Consciousness in the form of Kwan Yin. (Before she had simply visualised a brilliant light.) The image of Kwan Yin had a powerful effect on Amanda's mind. It brought an amount of mental sharpness to her that was new and the incidences of 'mental fog' decreased. Simultaneously, Amanda felt that she found more of her 'true self' – a deep, inner sense of love and security that was not conditioned by anything outside herself.

Summary
The ultimate healing-symbol is the symbol of your Higher Consciousness itself. We need to visualise our Higher Consciousness in a beautiful and radiantly colourful form.

You can work with the symbol of your Higher Consciousness in exactly the same way as you work with your other healing-symbols.

Working with the symbol of our Higher Consciousness will help you towards realising the unconditional happiness of your true nature.

Chapter 18
Manifesting our dreams

Most people find that their problems and negative emotions readily decrease once they work with the loving light of their healing-symbol. Once we have reached 1 or 2 on the scale of suffering, it is time to start working on manifesting our dreams. How to do this is described in a huge number of self-help books which have become very popular in recent years. Unfortunately, despite this popularity, many people struggle to put these teachings into practice. Having used these techniques with great success myself over the past twenty years, I will try to clarify the most important points.

The core of manifesting our dreams is that we *trust that our wishes will manifest*. To do this, we need to suspend our ordinary ideas about time and space. It is not enough to simply visualise our dreams or think positively – even though this will be helpful. To build genuine trust, we need to spend time in which we genuinely experience that we *already have* what we wish for. This is a subtle but decisive difference from doing a visualisation exercise. For example, if we wish to find a partner, we should speak in our mind with this person and deeply enjoy our loving exchange. If we wish for success in our career, we should deeply enjoy the feeling of satisfaction that results from making other people happy with our products.

The next prerequisite for the successful manifestation of our dreams is to have a happy and loving mind. Unfortunately, feelings like resentment, guilt and victim mentality seem to work as an insurmountable barrier to fulfilling our desires. For example, we can try to visualise a soulmate or a successful career for a very long time but if we are full of bitterness and despair, we are unlikely to get anywhere with this technique. Therefore, if we are engulfed in negative emotions, it is paramount to reduce those feelings first with a healing-symbol before we can expect to get good results from visualising our aims.

Combining our aims with altruistic love

In principle, achieving our aims is extremely simple. It can be summarised in one single sentence: *Clearly define your aim and focus on it in an ongoing way.* Unfortunately, despite this simplicity, most people experience a host of obstacles when they are confronted with an unfulfilled desire. They may feel undeserving, they may feel hopeless or they may feel underconfident. They may also think that their wish is unrealistic, they may not believe in the power of their mind or they may even believe that focusing on their wish is selfish and sinful. Above all, they may feel very impatient, which is a subtle form of anger. Luckily, for all these obstacles, there is one single remedy. This remedy is love.

The key to successful manifestation is to combine our personal desires with altruistic love for all beings. For example, instead of simply wishing to have a successful business, we should concentrate on the wish to benefit all beings with our products. In that way, our own success will be a welcome 'by-product'. Instead of simply wishing for a partner, we should wish for becoming such a loving couple that our happiness will make many other people happy, as well. Obviously, in that way, we will also find a gorgeous partner.

Altruistic love will help us to fulfil our wishes more quickly because wishing for *everybody* will dissolve our feelings of unworthiness, impatience and doubts. Instead, we will feel more confident, deserving and powerful. It is exactly this empowered state of mind that makes it most likely that our wishes will be fulfilled. Moreover, wishing with love protects us from going on a selfish ego-trip and wishing for things that cannot bring happiness. For example, most people realise that simply being rich and famous does not bring any happiness as such. We just need to open any celebrity magazine to see that many rich and famous people have terrible problems. But living in a state of altruistic love will make us *very* happy, no matter what we do for a living.

The technique for manifesting our dreams
In preparation: Define your wish

Write down *as clearly and in as much detail as possible what you want to achieve. If other people are involved in your aim, remember that they have free will. Simply wish for them to be happy and do not impose your wishes on them.*

Make sure *that you have as much to give as you want to have. For example, if you wish for a very loving partner, make sure that you are very loving yourself. If you want to earn a large amount of money by selling a certain product, make sure that your product is worth this amount of money.*

Think of *as many ways as possible of how you can benefit others with the fulfilment of your wish. Write all this down.*

In relaxation: Focus on the reality of your fulfilled dream

When you go through the following steps, feel that they are really true in this present moment. Deeply enjoy the experience. Do not think that this is a visualisation exercise for something to manifest in the future.

Close your eyes, relax and generate a positive and happy feeling in yourself. Focus on this positive feeling until you feel really joyful.

Perceive yourself as beautiful and radiantly healthy. Really enjoy your body (do not think that you are merely imagining it).

Radiate love to everybody around you. Really feel the loving feeling.

Focus on the reality that all aspects of your wish are fulfilled in this present moment. See yourself in your ideal situation that contains, in symbolic form, all aspects of your wish. (For example, see yourself in a beautiful home, surrounded by loving relationships, with tokens of your achievement, an open bank statement that shows financial success, flight tickets for your travels, etc.)

See yourself surrounded by all the people you want to benefit with your wish (for example, happy customers, patients, clients, children, family members, friends, students, etc.).

See your Higher Consciousness above the entire scene, blessing it with a loving smile. Deeply enjoy this experience and see it as complete reality. Stay in this experience for as long as you like.

We need to work with these images every day for at least 5 to 10 minutes. In fact, the more we can think about our aim, the better. If we focus in the right way, we will feel as happy as if we have already received our wish.

We may be lucky and receive the fulfilment of our wish in a matter of weeks but in most cases, we will have to be more patient to see results. It is just this waiting time that can bring up many negative feelings like hopelessness, impatience or even despair. If this happens, we can work once again with Higher Consciousness Healing to dissolve these painful emotions. As I have said before, the manifestation technique will only bring results if we can focus on our aim *long term* while staying in a reasonably positive state of mind throughout. In fact, the happier we are, the more quickly our wish can be fulfilled but the more negative emotions we experience, the longer it will take.

It is also very important to stay with the same aim throughout. This situation can be compared with sowing seeds. If we sow one seed one day only to dig it up repeatedly and replace with another seed, we will never manage to harvest the fruits.

Finally, we need to do everything that common sense dictates to achieve our aim. For example, if we wish for a partner, it does not make sense to stay at home and watch television every day. Equally, if we want to become a successful artist, it will not happen by visualising alone. We also have to practise, attend schools and try to exhibit our works.

My own experiences with manifestation techniques
I am a big fan of manifestation techniques and have been using them with great success for over 35 years. In the beginning, my

results were slow and not very impressive because I did not truly believe in the power of my mind. Also, I didn't know any better and gave in to my negative feelings as and when they arose. All this changed when I experienced a shocking betrayal by my boyfriend that jolted me out of my self-pitying complacency. The extreme pain of this experience slowly transformed into a steely determination to only ever have a 'good' relationship. Four years later (it felt like an eternity at the time), I met my future husband and he became my deeply beloved soulmate. From then on, I didn't allow any aspect of my life to develop by chance. Career, family, home, emotions, health and spiritual development – I have had very precise aims for all these areas and I still do. Over the years, I have been able to 'tick off' wish after wish while being able to benefit more and more people in the process. For example, Higher Consciousness Healing is the result of my wish to find an extraordinarily effective therapeutic technique that has the potential to benefit everyone. The ongoing positive feedback from my clients and readers continues to make me deeply happy and grateful.

Summary
Once you have reduced your suffering to 1 or 2 on the scale with Higher Consciousness Healing, you can start manifesting your positive aims.
Always combine your personal aims with the wish to benefit all beings in the process.
Define your wish as clearly as possible and construct a key image that contains all aspects of your wish.

Focus on your aim as a reality that already exists. Deeply enjoy this experience and do not treat this as a visualisation exercise for things to manifest in the future.

Focus on your aim every day and be as patient and positive as possible. If strong negative emotions arise, use Higher Consciousness Healing to dissolve them.

Do everything that common sense dictates to achieve your aim.

Chapter 19
Practising Higher Consciousness Healing on behalf of others

Higher Consciousness Healing offers us a unique and highly effective technique that we can use to help our loved ones and the world in general. Before I explain in detail how to do this, let me first share one of the results that my client Barbara has achieved by helping herself, her husband and her daughter with Higher Consciousness Healing.

Case study: Barbara
Barbara contacted me because she was on the brink of divorce from her husband. They argued every day and their sex life was non-existent. I showed Barbara how to send love to herself and to her husband with the help of a healing-symbol. When she came back, she reported that she had stopped arguing with her husband and that she was able to value him more. She had also been able to be more assertive about some long-standing issues and had achieved a good compromise. Another two weeks on, Barbara told me that she and her husband had fallen in love again and that their sex life had been rekindled. Obviously, her husband was over the moon even though he didn't know anything about Higher Consciousness Healing (Barbara had feared he might find this practice too weird and threatening).

In the next step, Barbara told me about the terrible tantrums of her four-year-old son that drove her mad. She received a healing-symbol (a light blue child's bed) and practised it for another two weeks on behalf of her son. She visualised him in front of her inner eye and saw the blue child's bed in his heart.

Then she imagined the blue light radiating into his little body and all around him, filling him with love. To her joy, her son improved dramatically and only rarely had a tantrum from then on. All these improvements were stable and lasting.

Before considering practising Higher Consciousness Healing on behalf of others

Generally speaking, *we should only practise Higher Consciousness Healing on behalf of someone else if we feel loving and positive towards this person.* By contrast, if we feel negative emotions towards the other person, we should work on our *own* painful feelings first. For example, if we are annoyed that our partner is miserable and depressed, we should first work with a symbol on *our own* annoyance. Often, this will already have a healing effect on our partner. It is important to understand that this change does not come about through some sort of secret manipulation but through the working of our Higher Consciousness, which always acts in the best interest of everybody concerned. Once we feel loving and positive towards the other person, we can help them by practising Higher Consciousness Healing on their behalf as described below.

Case study: Sheila

Sheila had not properly communicated with her adult son in years. She had worried a lot about him and had successfully reduced this negative feeling with a healing-symbol. When she talked to me, she felt more confident and peaceful but her son was just as withdrawn and miserable as before. So she decided to use a healing-symbol on his behalf and practised it with all her heart. To her extreme surprise, her son came to her house a few days later and voluntarily started to talk about his problems – something he had never done before. Sheila was overjoyed and from then on their relationship improved a great deal.

There are three different ways that we can use Higher Consciousness Healing to help others.

Joining someone else in their practice of Higher Consciousness Healing

We can help someone else who is already working with a healing-symbol by joining in with their practice. Firstly, we need to ask this person which healing-symbol they have received from their Higher Consciousness and listen carefully to the description. Then we need to visualise the person we want to help in front of us and see or sense *their* healing-symbol in *their* heart. When we breathe out, we visualise the colour of their symbol radiating out from their heart and filling their body and their whole surroundings with love. Love means wishing this person to be happy and healthy with all your heart. We do this for two minutes twice a day for two weeks - exactly as we would with our own symbol. In my experience, if two friends or a couple work together in this way, the results of Higher Consciousness Healing can be even more dramatic.

Practising Higher Consciousness Healing on behalf of another person with their consent

Generally speaking, it is better to *teach* others the simple practice of Higher Consciousness Healing because helping people to help themselves is the most empowering support. However, in some cases, people feel too weak, ill or - in the case of children - they may be too young to work with Higher Consciousness Healing. In these cases, the other person may be very grateful if we offer to practise Higher Consciousness Healing on their behalf. To do this, we first need to clarify what emotion the other person wants to overcome - as described in Chapter 5: Defining our problem. Then we can ask our own Higher Consciousness for a healing-symbol on behalf of the other person. Once we are relaxed, we should ask in the following way:

Higher Consciousness, can you please give me a healing-symbol for (name) that will help her/him to overcome her/his suffering from feeling (anger, sadness, anxiety) about...

In the next step, we practise the healing-symbol on behalf of the other person as I have described in the previous section.

Once children are of school age, we can start to teach them how to use Higher Consciousness Healing themselves. In the beginning, we may still have to ask for a symbol on their behalf but we can make a simple drawing of the symbol and ask them to join us in the visualisation. As the child grows older, they will be able to do more and more Higher Consciousness Healing by themselves.

The other person does not know that we practise Higher Consciousness Healing on their behalf

In some cases, it is impossible to ask people to consent to us practising Higher Consciousness Healing on their behalf. For instance, sometimes, we deeply care for a family member but we have never talked to them about their personal problems. We may also fear that the other person may reject Higher Consciousness Healing. In all these cases, we can still practise Higher Consciousness Healing on behalf of others and we can be assured that our practice will only work in the highest interest of the other person. As long as we ask our Higher Consciousness for a healing-symbol and use it with love, there is no danger of imposing our personal will on other people. As I have explained before, we all share our Higher Consciousness even though it may appear to us in many different forms and shapes.

Practising Higher Consciousness Healing on behalf of small children is extremely rewarding. To my joy, I have witnessed how children have slept through the night for the first time in years and how they have stopped having tantrums, becoming happy and co-operative, instead.

When we work with Higher Consciousness Healing on behalf of others, we should ask for a healing-symbol and practise it as outlined in the previous two sections. If we do not know from which negative emotion our friend or relative suffers, we can simply ask for a healing-symbol to help the other person to overcome 'their unhappiness'.

Case study: Jake
The mother of four-year-old Jake contacted me because her son was very afraid of going to school. He was still attending nursery but he always became very emotional when his parents tried to talk to him about his impending change to primary school. His parents had promised him a lovely present for his first day at

school but it didn't help. Therefore, I helped Jake's mother to receive a healing-symbol on his behalf to overcome his anxiety. She received a bright red toy fireman as a symbol. After practising it for a week, she drove past Jake's primary school and said, as usual, what a lovely school it was. To her immense surprise, Jake announced confidently that this was his favourite school and that he was looking forward to going there in the summer. From then on, Jake's fear of going to school disappeared.

Summary

You need to feel positive and loving towards someone who you want to help with Higher Consciousness Healing. If you are involved in the problem, you need to dissolve your own negative emotions first.

You can join others in their practice of Higher Consciousness Healing to increase their results.

If you practise Higher Consciousness Healing on behalf of others, ask for a symbol in the following way: 'Higher Consciousness, can you please give me a healing-symbol for (name) that will help her/him to overcome her/his suffering from feeling (anger, sadness, anxiety) about...'

Visualise the person that you want to help in front of you and see their symbol in their heart radiating healing light into their body and enveloping them in a bubble of love.

Chapter 20
Teaching Higher Consciousness Healing to others

Would you like to pass Higher Consciousness Healing on to your friends? Would you like to use Higher Consciousness Healing in your counselling practice or teach this method in evening classes and workshops? You can – you have my explicit permission to do this. However, to be a confident teacher of Higher Consciousness Healing, I would like to ask you to achieve at least two real personal successes with this method with your own problems. 'Real' success means that you have practised Higher Consciousness Healing on two personal issues in exactly the way I have described in this book and that you should score no more than one or two on the scale of suffering as a result. Your life-path imagery should also have 'improved' accordingly. With your own success in the back of your mind, you will be an empathic counsellor who radiates genuine optimism and you will be a teacher who can inspire their students.

It is my deep wish that as many people as possible benefit from Higher Consciousness Healing and if you feel inspired by this method, you are warmly invited to support this aim. In my vision, I see people all over the globe solving their debilitating and crippling problems. I see children in school being taught this simple method and I see everybody much happier and more confident. Tiny sparks of light grow stronger, they grow together and spread. If we are happier and more loving as individuals, we will influence our whole environment in a positive way. We will bring peace and happiness into our families, to our workplaces, to our communities and finally to the whole world. It is a grand aim but we have to start with ourselves.

When you pass Higher Consciousness Healing on to others, I would like to ask you not to change this method in any way. Even the smallest details are important. Also, if you use Higher Consciousness Healing with your clients, you should always make them aware that this is a self-help method that they can use on their own as soon as they are ready. Sadly, I once met a therapist who had learnt Higher Consciousness Healing from this book but only gave his clients symbols that he had asked for on their behalf. Working in this way may be good for his earnings because it makes his clients more dependent on him but it is not truly empowering. I also found a website advertising this method and it offered symbols for people to use without giving credit to this book. This is not how I want people to spread this method. Please make sure that you pass on Higher Consciousness Healing in the self-help spirit in which it is intended.

Study groups and self-help groups are more great ways of practising Higher Consciousness Healing together. Self-help groups are very empowering because they give everyone the additional boost of confidence that comes from being able to help themselves.

You can start a self-help group by just meeting with one friend. I am sure that after only a short time, your work will attract some more friends who will want to find out why you are suddenly able to solve one problem in your life after another. Here are some suggestions for running a self-help group:

Rotate the leadership of the group every time you meet.
Use this book or a tape recording to guide you through the practice to receive new symbols.

Share your experiences with Higher Consciousness Healing and listen to each other but do not give advice to each other unless someone explicitly asks for it.

May all your problems be resolved. I wish you the best of luck.

Chapter 21
The complete practice of Higher Consciousness Healing

Part one: Preparation
Identify *the negative emotion around your problem and define your problem in the form of: 'My suffering from feeling (anger, sadness, anxiety, etc.) about...' (WRITE THIS DEFINITION DOWN.)*
Measure *on a scale from 0 to 10 how much, on average, you are suffering from the negative emotion (anger, sadness, anxiety) about your problem (0 is no suffering at all, 5 is a good deal of suffering, at 7 despair starts and 10 is utter desperation). (WRITE THIS NUMBER DOWN.)*
Ask someone *to read out to you the following exercise or make your own tape.*
Prepare *to go into relaxation.*

Part two: Receiving symbols in relaxation (tape this part or ask a friend to read it out to you)
Relaxation
Sit or *lie down comfortably and undo all tight clothing. You can put your hands on your stomach to feel the movement of your breathing. Every time you breathe in, you feel your hands slightly rise and every time you breathe out, you feel your hands slightly fall.... Let yourself fall into the out-breath and relax your whole being....*
You are *now going on a journey through your whole body. Start with your feet. Bring your awareness into your feet and feel inside your feet. Let all tensions fall away with your out-breath.... Now*

feel into your lower legs and let all tensions fall away with your out-breath.... And now do the same with your thighs... your abdomen... your stomach... your chest... your shoulders... your arms... your neck... your face... your whole head.... Your whole being is now wonderfully relaxed... enjoy that feeling....

And now *you sink even more deeply into relaxation and, as I count from one to ten, you see yourself going down a stairway towards a beautiful and secure place. As I say each number, you take one step down – sinking deeper and deeper into relaxation: one, two, deeper and deeper... three, four, deeper still... five, six, seven, deeper... eight, and deeper... nine, ten.... You have now arrived at your beautiful place and you are completely safe here. Find somewhere to make yourself comfortable.*

Meeting your Higher Consciousness

You are *now ready to contact your Higher Consciousness. This is the part of yourself that is completely loving and wise and already knows the answers to all your questions. At the same time, it is outside yourself and you share it with everybody else. Your personal Higher Consciousness is also the Higher Consciousness of the whole universe. You can imagine it as a living, shimmering light or as an angelic being surrounded by brilliant light or as the central figure of the religion you follow.*

See and *feel your Higher Consciousness coming nearer to you. You can feel how its beams of love surround you and care for you and you can sense how you yourself become more loving and joyful when you are touched by the wonderful presence of your Higher Consciousness. Your Higher Consciousness is a symbol of your highest potential. To move towards it and finally unite with* *it is both your ultimate task and your goal in life. Doing this will bring you the kind of joy and happiness that does not depend on outer conditions and cannot be taken away from you.*

Exploration of your life-path (optional)

Now see *your Higher Consciousness on top of a mountain and ask it to show you a path, a track or a road leading towards the mountaintop.*

Now ask *your Higher Consciousness: 'Can you please show me where I am on this path?'*

When you *have received the answer, remember that it does not matter whether you are still down in the valley or whether you are already halfway up the mountain. All that matters is that you are moving towards your Higher Consciousness and that you are unfolding its wonderful qualities.*

Now ask *your Higher Consciousness to show you what you are doing on your life-path when you experience your problem. For example, you may be straying from your path, walking on the spot or going downhill. Whatever is shown to you, do not judge yourself. Ask your Higher Consciousness in the following way: 'Can you please show me what I am doing on my life-path when I suffer from feeling (emotion) about...?'*

Thank your *Higher Consciousness for the answer.*

Asking for your healing-symbol

Now ask *your Higher Consciousness to show you a healing-symbol to overcome your problem. It could be something like a gemstone, a flower or a geometrical form. You may be shown one or several symbols and you should pick the one which feels best* for you. It needs to have a beautiful form and colour. Ask in the following way: 'Higher Consciousness, can you please give me a healing-symbol to overcome my suffering from feeling (emotion) about...'

If you like the symbol, thank your Higher Consciousness. If you do not like the symbol, ask for another one.

Working with your symbol

Now see or sense your healing-symbol in the openness of your heart in the middle of your chest. While you breathe out, radiate the colour and the positive qualities of your healing-symbol throughout your whole body and surround it with a bubble of loving, joyful light the size of your outstretched arms. It is a loving and healing light that brings comfort, clarity and happiness. Feel all tensions and negative emotions melting away in the loving light of your symbol. Wish yourself to be happy with all your heart. When you breathe in, just relax into the positive feeling that comes from seeing or feeling your healing-symbol in your heart. Then exhale its positive qualities again.

(If you find it difficult to send love to yourself, think first about someone you find easy to love and wish them to be happy. Without changing this feeling, turn it towards yourself and wish yourself to be happy with all your heart.)

If other people are involved in your problem, breathe the colour to them as well. See (name of the person) in front of you and feel how the loving, joyful light from your healing-symbol forms a bubble of love around them. Your own bubble of light may touch their bubble but they should not overlap. In your mind, say to this person, 'I wish you to be happy.' Know that everybody who is *genuinely happy would immediately repent their wrongdoing and become very likeable. If you feel resentment towards your parents, always send the loving light of your healing-symbol to them, as well. (If you feel guilty towards this person, say, 'I am sorry for what I did. I wish you to be happy'.)*

Notice if *you still feel any negative emotion. If yes, notice where in your physical body you feel the tensions that go along with this negative emotion.*

Direct *the healing light of your symbol to the part of your body where you feel the tensions of your negative emotion and relax these tensions with each out-breath. You can imagine these tensions as a tight flower bud that opens into a beautiful bloom with each out-breath.*

Sometimes, *tensions are in more than one place in the body. Relax all these tensions one after the other until your whole body is completely relaxed and your negative emotions are completely dissolved.*

If you *feel any form of fear or anxiety, use the anti-anxiety breathing technique at the same time.*

If you *feel sad or depressed, practice with a smile on your face.*
When *you are ready, open your eyes.*

Part three: in daily life

Use Higher Consciousness Healing for two minutes twice daily for a minimum period of two weeks and *every* time your negative thoughts and feelings come up. Instead of dwelling on negative self-talk and painful emotions, put your mind *immediately* on your healing-symbol and breathe out the colour to surround yourself and others with bubbles of loving, joyful light.

Simultaneously, put a smile on your face and relax the tensions of your negative emotions. Continue to work in this way no matter if good or bad things happen and never change your symbol. At the same time, put into practice any insight on how to solve and improve your problem.

After two weeks, measure your improvements on the scale (use the precise definition of the problem) and tune into your life-path imagery to check if there are any improvements. Try to appreciate even the smallest decrease in suffering.

About the author

Tara Springett has accompanied thousands of clients in their journey and has successfully helped them to alleviate their emotional, mental and often also physical symptoms. Tara`s websites contain positive testimonials from hundreds of grateful clients who have experienced relief from their problems by working with her.

Tara holds an MA in Education and has trained in Gestalt therapy, body awareness therapy and transpersonal therapy. Since 1988, Tara has worked as a drug addiction counsellor, a youth counsellor and a general psychotherapist.

Since 1986, Tara has practised daily Buddhist meditation and spent many weeks in individual and group retreats. In 1997, she received the empowerment of her Buddhist teacher, Rigdzin Shikpo, to teach meditation. In 2002, she was also asked by her Buddhist teacher, His Eminence Garchen Rinpoche, to teach.

Tara is a successful author of numerous self-help books that apply Buddhist wisdom to all areas of life: relationships, emotional issues, nutrition, wish fulfilment and others.

Tara has an adult son and lives in a retreat house in Devon, England with her soulmate and husband Nigel. She can be contacted via tara@taraspringett.com

Printed in Great Britain
by Amazon